COACHING
3-5-2 TACTICS

125 TACTICAL SOLUTIONS & PRACTICES

WRITTEN BY

RENATO MONTAGNOLO

PUBLISHED BY

COACHING
3-5-2 TACTICS

125 TACTICAL SOLUTIONS & PRACTICES

First Published in English - February 2020 by SoccerTutor.com
First Published in Italian - September 2017 by Allenatore.net S.A.S.

info@soccertutor.com | www.SoccerTutor.com

UK: 0208 1234 007 | **US:** (305) 767 4443 | **ROTW:** +44 208 1234 007
ISBN: 978-1-910491-37-9

Author
Renato Montagnolo - Allenatore.net S.A.S.

Edited by
Alex Fitzgerald - SoccerTutor.com

Cover Design by
Alex Macrides, Think Out Of The Box Ltd.
Email: design@thinkootb.com Tel: +44 (0) 208 144 3550

Diagrams
Diagram designs by SoccerTutor.com. All the diagrams in this book have been created using SoccerTutor.com Tactics Manager Software available from *www.SoccerTutor.com*

Note: While every effort has been made to ensure the technical accuracy of the content of this book, neither the author nor publishers can accept any responsibility for any injury or loss sustained as a result of the use of this material.

CONTENTS

TRAINING SESSION 3: SWITCHING PLAY 120

TRAINING SESSION 4: PLAYING IN BEHIND THE DEFENSIVE LINE 126

TRAINING SESSION 5: COMBINED MOVEMENTS OF THE 2 FORWARDS 132

TRAINING SESSION 6: TRANSITION FROM ATTACK TO DEFENCE 137

TRAINING SESSION 7: AGGRESSIVE PRESSING 143

TRAINING SESSION 8: ORGANISATION OF THE DEFENSIVE LINE 148

COACH PROFILE: RENATO MONTAGNOLO

Renato Montagnolo
- UEFA 'B' Coaching Licence
- Reggio Audace (Serie C) Assistant Manager

- **COACHING QUALIFICATIONS AND EXPERIENCE:**

  » **UEFA 'B' Coaching Licence**

  » **Reggio Audace FC (Serie C) Assistant Manager and Match Analyst** (2019 - present)

  » **UC AlbinoLeffe (Serie C) Assistant Manager and Match Analyst** (2016 - 2018)

  » **A.S.D. Jolly Montemurlo Junior Team Manager and First Team Match Analyst** (2015 - 2016)

- **FOOTBALL COACHING BOOK AUTHOR:**

  » **Defensive Line: Organisational and Educational Principles** - with Francesco Farioli, www.allenatore.net, Lucca 2016.

  » **4-2-3-1: Tactical Solutions for Positional Football** - www.allenatore.net, Lucca 2019.

- **FOOTBALL TACTICS AND MATCH ANALYSIS EXPERT:**

  » **Patentino Match Analyst Licence** - awarded with 101/110 grade in July 2018.

  » **First Team Match Analyst** at Reggio Audace FC (Serie C), UC AlbinoLeffe (Serie C) and A.S.D. Jolly Montemurlo.

  » **Writer and Collaborator** for www.allenatore.net, New Football Print Magazine and obiettivorganitecture.it page: "Objective Organisation: Tactics and Methodology."

  » **Speaker and Teacher** for live web course "Tactical Timing: Principles and Teaching to Plan the Training Cycle and the Next Season."

  » **Speaker and Teacher** for tactical conferences, such as "A.S.D. Polisportiva Prato Nord 1v1: Attention to Detail to Train the Defender," AIAC Bergamo, A.S.D. Polisportiva Prato Nord: "Train the Defence: From Individual Tactics to Collective Tactics."

INTRODUCTION

The aim of this books is to provide a series of ideas and useful information for all those interested in gaining a thorough knowledge of the 3-5-2 system of play.

The 3-5-2 formation has been deemed by many to be a defensive system, but this is not the case. A system of play is not universally attacking or defensive - it is the interpretation of the coach that determines the characteristics of the team's play.

This book outlines the 3-5-2 formation as an expansive possession based system, which focuses on playing through the lines of the opposition and utilises the wing backs as an attacking outlet in wide areas.

CHAPTER 1: TACTICAL STRENGTHS AND WEAKNESSES OF THE 3-5-2 FORMATION

In the first chapter, we provide an analysis of the 3-5-2 system, with reference to the strengths and weaknesses in the attacking and defensive phases.

CHAPTER 2: 3-5-2 TACTICS AGAINST DIFFERENT FORMATIONS

The main part of the book (chapter 2) is focused on examining the 3-5-2 system against many different formations in both phases:

- 4-4-2
- 4-2-3-1
- 4-3-3
- 4-3-1-2
- 3-5-2
- 3-4-3

For the attacking phase, 3 different situations are examined:

1. **Overcoming the First Line of Pressing (Build-up Play from the Back)**
2. **Moving the Ball in Between the Opposition's Midfield and Defensive Lines**
3. **Playing in Behind the Opposition's Defensive Line**

For the defensive phase, 2 different situations are examined:

1. **Pressing and Defensive Organisation**
2. **Organisation of the Defensive Line**

CHAPTER 3: TRAINING SESSION EXAMPLES

Finally, in the last chapter, we organise our 3-5-2 tactical practices into 8 specific training sessions:

1. **Build-up Play from the Back**
2. **Playing Through the Lines**
3. **Switching Play**
4. **Playing in Behind the Defensive Line**
5. **Combined Movements of the 2 Forwards**
6. **Transition from Attack to Defence**
7. **Aggressive Pressing**
8. **Organisation of the Defensive Line**

Coach's at all levels can use these practices with their team and adjust them according to the conditions they have (time, space, characteristics of the players etc.)

COACHING FORMAT

I. TACTICAL ANALYSIS AND SOLUTIONS

- Renato Montagnolo is a tactics and match analyst expert. He has provided analysis and tactical solutions for the 3-5-2 formation in different game situations against different formations.

- Each action, pass, individual movement (with or without the ball) and the positioning of each player on the pitch including their body shape, are presented with a full description.

2. TRAINING SESSIONS

- Technical and Functional Unopposed Practices

- Functional and Tactical Opposed Practices

- Small Sided Games / Conditioned Games

- Tactical 11v11 Games

- Name/Objective, Full Description, Conditions, Variations, Progressions & Rules (if applicable)

KEY

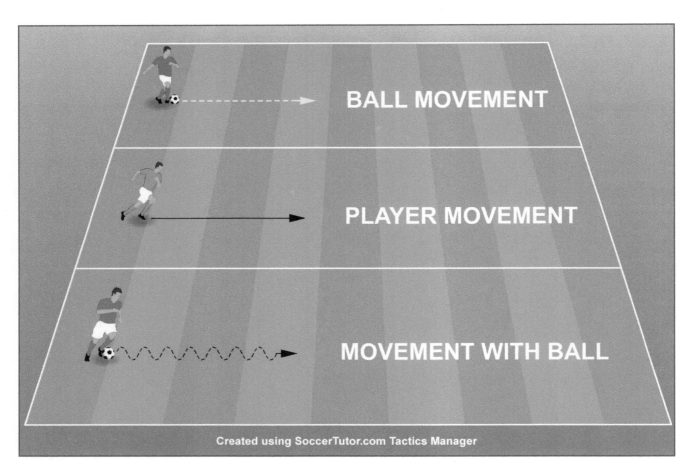

BALL MOVEMENT

PLAYER MOVEMENT

MOVEMENT WITH BALL

Created using SoccerTutor.com Tactics Manager

CHAPTER I

TACTICAL STRENGTHS AND WEAKNESSES OF THE 3-5-2 FORMATION

TACTICAL STRUCTURE OF THE 3-5-2 FORMATION

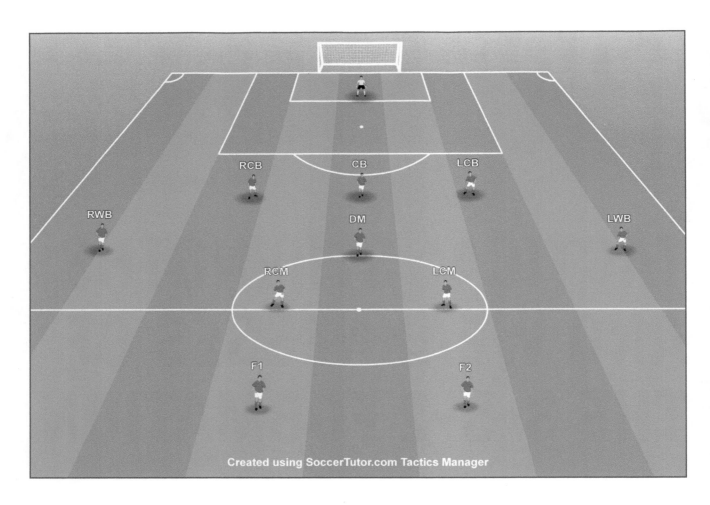

Created using SoccerTutor.com Tactics Manager

- **RCB:** Right Centre Back

- **CB:** Middle Centre Back

- **LCB:** Left Centre Back

- **RWB:** Right Wing Back

- **LWB:** Left Wing Back

- **DM:** Defensive Midfielder

- **RCM:** Right Central Midfielder

- **LCM:** Left Central Midfielder

- **F1:** Forward 1

- **F2:** Forward 2

IDEAL CHARACTERISTICS FOR PLAYERS IN THE 3-5-2 FORMATION

MIDDLE CENTRE BACK (CB)

- Strong personality to lead the defensive line.

- Tactically intelligent.

- Ability to read game situations and anticipate, especially when covering the space in behind the defensive line.

- Good physical structure.

- Good technique to play out from the back.

- Ability to play short (15-20 yards).

- Ability to play long passes (switch play to the wing back).

WIDE CENTRE BACKS (LCB / RCB)

- Ability to read game situations and anticipate.

- Strong defenders that are good in 1 v 1 situations.

- Must be fast and able to shift across quickly.

- Good quality and fundamental technique to overcome the first line of pressing.

- Fluidity in playing out from the back.

- Comfortable receiving and moving forward with the ball (and favour this approach).

- Preferably have a right footed and left footed wide centre back in the team (balance).

- Attacking threat in the air from set-pieces.

WING BACKS (LWB / RWB)

- Extremely fit (high conditioning levels).

- Good progression with and without the ball.

- Strong in defending 1 v 1 situations.

- Good at attacking in 1 v 1 situations, which is fundamental in creating a numerical superiority in the attacking phase.

- Equipped with the necessary technique to receive and cross into dangerous areas as quickly as possible.

DEFENSIVE MIDFIELDER (DM)

- Must be a player of personality, able to drive the team.

- Tactically intelligent and able to read all different game situations.

- Adapt his position on the pitch, depending on the development of the opposition's attack.

- Does not have to be a big/tall player, as the marking in the penalty area is almost guaranteed to be covered by the 3 centre backs.

- Dynamic player.

- Able to quickly press (forward and sideways) and block passing lanes.

- Excellent applied technique.

- Ability to play short (15-20 yards).

- Ability to play long passes (switch play to the wing back).

- Adept at creating space and angles to receive in behind the opposition's first line of pressing.

- Ability to play forward and through the lines, accelerating the development of the game by bypassing the midfield and, in some cases, even the defensive line of the opponents.

CENTRAL MIDFIELDERS (LCM / RCM)

- Dynamic players who are extremely fit (high conditioning levels).

- Must be able to make medium and long sprints to press their opponents.

- Must be able to cover large areas of the pitch during the defensive phase (out of possession).

- Make incisive runs to attack the space in behind the opposition's defensive line.

- Good attacking 1 v 1 skills.

- From their central midfielders, the team requires an ability to play final passes in the final third to create goal scoring opportunities and an ability to contain their opponents.

- Ideally, the team would have 1 central midfielder that is strong and more defensive-minded and another who is more technical, refined and attack-minded.

- Both central midfielders must be tactically intelligent and coordinate their movements with the wing backs.

- Capable of shooting and scoring from outside the penalty area.

FORWARDS (F1 / F2)

- The 2 forwards should have complementary characteristics and abilities.

- One of the forwards must be quick and able to exploit the space in behind the opposition's defensive line with good runs.

- The other forward must be a player capable of connecting with the midfielders and wing backs to bring the team into the finishing zone - this can be a strong player who receives with his back to goal or a more mobile player able to create space and receive between the lines.

- Tactically disciplined players able to play with combined movements.

- Good at exploiting crosses that come from outside the penalty area.

1. ATTACKING PHASE

STRENGTHS AND WEAKNESSES OF THE 3-5-2 IN THE ATTACKING PHASE

STRENGTHS

- There are many possibilities and solutions when building up play and constructing attacks by using diamond shapes.

- The first diamond shape is created with the goalkeeper (**GK**) and the 3 defenders (**LCB**, **CB** & **RCB**).

- The second diamond shape is created with the 3 defenders and the defensive midfielder (**DM**).

- The 2 wing backs (**LWB** & **RWB**) are always available and ready to contribute in the attacking phase.

- The presence of 2 centre forwards (**F1** & **F2**) allows many different combination solutions, making it difficult for the opposing defenders.

- Possibility for combined movements between the defensive midfielder (**DM**) and the other 2 central midfielders (**LCM** & **RCM**).

- The midfield is spaced out, which allows for various different passing solutions.

WEAKNESSES

- The space between the opposition's midfield and defensive lines is not occupied by any player's initial position.

- The wide areas are only initially occupied by 1 player, thus reducing the chances of combination play on the flanks.

1.1 - THE 3 CENTRE BACKS (LCB, CB & RCB)

The 3-5-2 is often wrongly thought of as a "defensive" game system, as people focus on the advantage of having 3 centre backs with the characteristics of pure defenders. However, this neglects the advantages that the 3 centre backs guarantee you in the possession phase.

In a more and more tactically evolved football, playing 3 at the back offers the possibility of organising a fluid possession phase with a numerical superiority right from the initial build-up play. This happens without having to over-modify the static positions of the players on the pitch.

BUILD-UP PLAY

When playing with a back 4, many teams have to drop their defensive midfielder between the 2 centre backs when building up play. When playing with a back 3 in the build-up phase, you usually avoid having to involve the defensive midfielder in deep areas.

With the defensive midfielder positioned higher up the pitch, the centre backs look to find a passing lane and are able to cut through the first line of pressing by passing forward to him.

If you have 3 centre backs and a defensive midfielder, the coach will have to teach his players to read the various ways opponents can press and develop them to adjust their passing patterns to play through them and into midfield.

As we will see in detail in the following chapter ("Chapter 2: Tactics Against Different Formations"), a team that builds up play with 3 centre backs will have to be able to exploit their numerical superiority in deep areas effectively.

When using the 3-5-2 formation, the 3 centre backs must be able to take advantage of any static numerical superiority against opponents

who structure their pressing with 1 or 2 forwards. In this situation, it will be necessary to have the option of a defender dribbling the ball forward into space.

Against teams that structure their pressing with 3 players up against the 3 centre backs (numerical equality), a dynamic numerical superiority can be created with the involvement of the goalkeeper or the defensive midfielder. As we will see in detail later in the book, both ways use combined movements of the central midfielders and wing backs to create passing lanes behind the opposition's first line of pressing and towards the free man.

1.2 - THE 2 WING BACKS (LWB & RWB)

The 3-5-2 formation includes 2 wing backs, that consistently ensure maximum width for the team. A coach who decides to use the 3-5-2 formation must try to make the most of these 2 players, who stand near the side line during the attacking (possession) phase.

Against teams that tend to close the central spaces, teams playing with the 3-5-2 rely on their wing backs to be the main attacking outlet. For this reason, as mentioned and emphasised earlier, these players must have certain 1 v 1 attacking skills and characteristics and good quality technique, which are all fundamental to creating a numerical superiority during the possession phase of the game.

EXPLOITING SPACE OUT WIDE

In general, almost all teams aim to narrow the spaces and have a high number of players in the centre of the pitch and around the ball zone during the defensive phase.

For this reason, a team using the 3-5-2 formation will often have the opportunity to move the ball to one of their wing backs in a situation of considerable advantage in their position.

They will have the space to receive the ball comfortably and time to play, especially against teams that play with a back 4.

This happens for 2 main reasons:

- The presence of many players in the central areas of the 3-5-2 forces opponents to adapt and close the spaces centrally.

- The presence of 2 forwards in the 3-5-2 forces the opposition's defensive line to tighten, making sure not to allow a 2 v 2 situation to develop in the centre of their defence.

To exploit this advantage, therefore, the team that plays with the 3-5-2 should:

1. Look for attacks on the weak side (especially if the opposing full backs are positioned close to their centre backs).

2. Force the opposing players to shift from one area of the pitch to another quickly.

Forcing the opposing players to shift from one area of the pitch to another quickly provides a high probability of the opposition losing their initial compactness and allows for more space and gaps to exploit with forward attacking movement.

This leads to isolating defenders, therefore creating and exploiting frontal 1 v 1 situations. It also creates gaps in the opposition's defensive organisation, which can be exploited by playing in behind their defensive line.

1.3 - THE 3 MIDFIELDERS (DM, LCM & RCM)

The 3 midfielders in the 3-5-2 formation ensure a good staggered midfield and allow the team to have various game solutions.

BUILD-UP PLAY

When building up play, the staggering of the 3 midfielders with a deep defensive midfielder allows you to have:

- The defensive midfielder positioned between the opposition's attacking and midfield line. He is the first player able to receive a pass that breaks through the first line of pressing.

- A "central midfielder," which we describe as the left or right central midfielder in this book, can make combined movements (inside, outside and laterally), can open up to receive and help overcome the opposition's first pressing line.

If the opponents are good at closing the passing lanes towards the defensive midfielder, the presence of 3 midfielders can allow both a rotation and a simple interchange of positions, all aimed at creating a passing lane for the opposite central midfielder to receive between the opposition's attacking and midfield lines.

COMBINATION PLAY BETWEEN THE LINES

There are no immediate solutions in the static 3-5-2 formation to receive between the lines. Progressing the attack relies on the left and right central midfielders moving to occupy the space between the opposition's midfield and defensive lines.

The left or right central midfielder has to move behind the opposition's midfielders to occupy a position which is not too deep or too high. If the central midfielder is too deep when receiving,

he will be easily pressed by one of the opposing midfielders. If he is too high, he will be absorbed by the defenders.

The <u>3 OPTIONS</u> for how to occupy the space between the lines with the 3-5-2:

1. The central midfielder who is considered more incisive to play in between the lines should always be positioned in there.

2. Alternatively, the central midfielder that is closest to the ball area or the opposite one is in there (depending on the coach's tactical strategy).

3. Both of the central midfielders are positioned in between the lines.

This third option should only be adopted if the team has a safe, fluid and stable defensive structure. Otherwise, it is preferable to keep at least one central midfielder in front of the opposition's midfield line to ensure greater balance in case possession is lost.

MIDFIELD ROTATION

The occupation of the space between the lines can also be the result of rotation between the dynamic central midfielders.

As we said, the space between the lines can be occupied in various ways, which could be strict patterns from the coach or can be left more to the interpretation of the players. In the latter case, the coach will have to establish a priority principle to establish:

1. Movement priorities (which sector to move the ball to, what space to occupy in our half, where the defensive midfielder is and what space to occupy in the opposition's half).

2. The number of players that must occupy the space between the opposition's lines.

1.4 - COMBINATION PLAY BETWEEN THE WING BACKS AND CENTRAL MIDFIELDERS

A big strength of the 3-5-2 formation is the combined movements between the central midfielders and the wing backs.

These are the best ways for these players to combine when using the 3-5-2:

- When building up play from the back, if the wing back (**LWB** or **RWB**) moves close to the ball in a deep position, the central midfielder on that side (**LCM** or **RCM**) has to move forward and try to receive the ball between the opposition's midfield and defensive lines.

- In contrast, if the wing back (**LWB** or **RWB**) moves forward and in between the opposition's midfield and defensive lines, the central midfielder (**LCM** or **RCM**) on that side has to drop back into a deeper position in front of the opposition's midfielders.

- When the wing back (**LWB** or **RWB**) receives the ball, the central midfielder (**LCM** or **RCM**) on that side has to read the game situation relative to how the opposition apply their pressing.

- If the opponents allow the wing back (**LWB** or **RWB**) space to dribble the ball, the central midfielder (**LCM** or **RCM**) on that side must attack the space created.

- If the opponents close down the wing back (**LWB** or **RWB**) and don't allow him to move with the ball, the central midfielder (**LCM** or **RCM**) on that side must move to create a passing angle and receive a short pass from the wing back, to maintain possession and build the attack.

KEY POINTS

- The combined movements of the wing backs and central midfielders is key to success in the attacking phase when using the 3-5-2 formation.

- The players need to concentrate at all times and make the right decision and movement based on the actions of their team-mate.

1.5 - THE 2 FORWARDS (F1 & F2)

Playing with 2 centre forwards (**F1** and **F2**) can be a great advantage, especially against teams that play with a back 4. The opposition are forced to make a choice:

1. Defend narrow and be vulnerable out wide.

2. Allow a 2v2 situation in the centre.

The way in which the 2 forwards are used depends on the needs of the coach, his tactical ideas and the players available. In general, we can make a distinction in 2 groups:

1. **Combined Movements** (can be horizontal or vertical but must play close to each other)

2. **Individual Movements** (can be horizontal or vertical but play apart from each other)

COMBINED MOVEMENTS

To encourage combined movements between the 2 centre forwards, it is first necessary that they play very close to each other.

When playing against a back 4, the 2 forwards must be in central positions, maintaining a 2v2 situation against the opposing centre backs.

When playing against a back 3, the 2 forwards will slightly shift their position close to the ball area and go up against the 2 closest defenders to maintain the same 2v2 situation.

In order for the combined movements to be effective, the following is needed:

- Make sure the players are able to read the specific tactical situation.

- Provide precise patterns for the players to follow for specific tactical situations, so they can react immediately and easily.

- The combinations need to be very quick, as there is reduced space in these areas.

- Quick combinations are very difficult for the opposing defenders to read and react.

- Establish signals which are recognised by all players. The team can then develop their movements automatically at the right times.

The attacking combination play starts when one of the forwards receives the ball.

We have analysed some possible combinations between 2 close forwards. To do this, we studied the **Italian National Team** at the **UEFA European Championships** in 2016 under **Antonio Conte**, who is one of the world's best coaches of the 3-5-2 formation.

We decided to analyse Conte's Italy because the two years of preparation for the European Championship was particularly focused on the importance of the 2 forwards and their combined movements.

There were 5 main combined movements and the analysis is displayed on the following pages...

I.6 - TACTICAL ANALYSIS OF ITALY FORWARDS' "COMBINED MOVEMENTS" AT UEFA EURO 2016

A. Drop Back, Dummy the Pass and Run in Behind (1)

Created using SoccerTutor.com Tactics Manager

NOTE: As we have said, the coach will have to provide precise patterns and signals for these combined movements in different game situations. This will help the forwards know which one should move away from their marker.

The attacking solution and combined movement most used by **Antonio Conte's Italy** using 2 forwards was for the deepest forward to move as if he's going to receive a short pass, but then let the ball run (dummy) to the more advanced forward, as long as there was enough pace on the ball.

This drags the defender forward and creates space in behind, which can then be exploited.

In this example shown above, the deepest forward moves to meet the ball and drags his marker with him, but then lets the ball run to the more advanced forward.

The deeper forward then quickly spins and runs forward, to move in behind his marker and receive the pass from his teammate.

B. Drop Back, Dummy the Pass and Run in Behind (2)

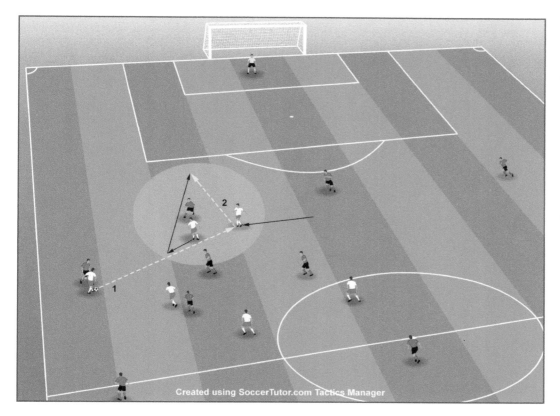

This is very similar to the previous example, but this time the pass is more horizontal and the forwards are on the left side of the pitch.

The deeper forward again spins (after dummy) and receives from his teammate in behind his marker.

C. Drop Back, Dummy the Pass and Receive Back

This is a variation of the previous 2 examples.

The forward's marker is not dragged forward (no space created in behind), so the forward receives back from his teammate instead and Italy simply maintain possession.

D. Opposite Vertical Movements to Create Space in Behind (1)

This combined movement of the forwards is used when a teammate has time on the ball.

One forward drops back as if to receive and drags his marker with him.

The midfielder passes into the space created in behind for the second forward to receive.

E. Opposite Vertical Movements to Create Space in Behind (2)

This is very similar to the previous example, but this time the pass is from a more central position and is played in between the 2 opposing centre backs.

The forward again receives in the space created in behind.

I.7 - TACTICAL SOLUTIONS FOR THE "COMBINED MOVEMENTS" OF THE FORWARDS

The fundamental aspects under consideration when deciding what combined movements to use are:

- Time and space available.
- Position of the ball.
- Position of team-mate.
- Amount of time team-mate has to play.

The forwards' combined movements can be developed with the pair starting:

- Horizontal to each other, with the closest player to the ball being the widest.
- Vertical to each other, with the closest player to the ball being the deepest.
- Diagonally angled to each other.

A. Dummy the Pass from the Side and Run in Behind

The ball is passed inside by the right wing back (**RWB**) towards the forwards.

The closest forward (**F1**) performs a dummy and lets the ball run to **F2**.

F1 decides whether or not to make a run in behind depending on the space available behind the red centre back. In this example, there is space and **F2** passes in behind to **F1**.

B. Dummy the Pass from the Side and Receive the Lay-off

This is a variation of the previous example (A).

There is not the same space to attack behind the red centre back, so **F1** receives the lay-off from **F2** instead of making a run in behind.

The blues maintain possession.

C. Drop Back to Create Space for Diagonal Pass in Behind

The closest forward to the ball (**F1**) drops back and drags his marker with him.

This creates a passing angle for the right wing back (**RWB**) and space for **F2** to receive the diagonal pass in behind the defensive line.

D. Moving Towards Central Midfielder who is Under Pressure

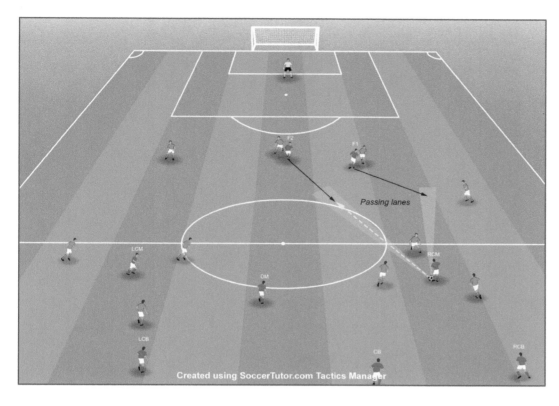

The central midfielder (**RCM**) is put under pressure by 3 red players.

The forwards (**F1** and **F2**) move towards him and into available passing lanes to try and receive.

F2 is able to receive from **RCM's** pass and the attack can progress.

E. Receive in Behind from Central Midfielder with Time on Ball

The right central midfielder (**RCM**) receives with time on the ball.

The closest forward (**F1**) drops back and drags his marker with him.

F2 makes a diagonal run into the space created and receives straight **RCM's** long pass in behind the defensive line.

F. Opposite Diagonal Movements to Receive Long Pass in Behind from the Centre Back

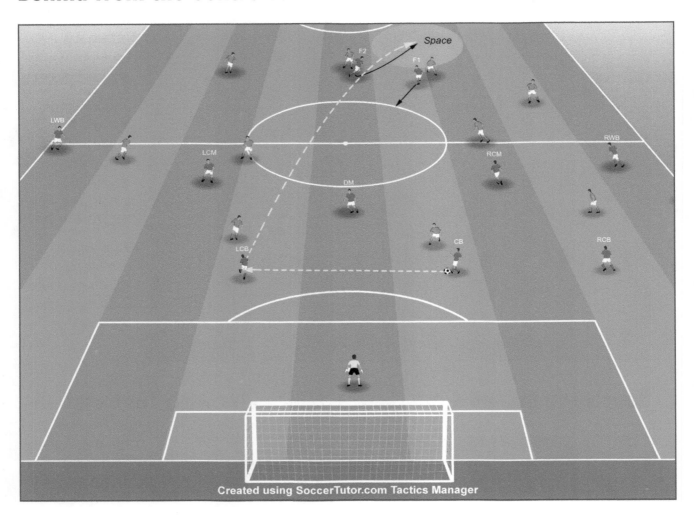

In this situation, the 2 forwards (**F1** and **F2**) are close and start level with each other. For this combined movement, their communication and understanding is key.

There also needs to be a clear signal between the centre back in possession and the forwards.

The left centre back (**LCB**) receives and one of the forwards (**F1** in diagram) drops back and drags his marker with him.

This creates space for **F2** to run into and the left centre back (**LCB**) plays a long pass in behind the defensive line.

1.8 - INDIVIDUAL MOVEMENTS OF THE FORWARDS

When 2 forwards are distant from each other, they cannot, at least at first, combine together. Their movements will mainly be individual ones. The collaboration between them will be dependent on receiving the ball with time to play.

Given the distance and the impossibility of performing combined movements (see previous pages), the 2 forwards (**F1** and **F2**) have to try to find different ways of creating difficulties for their direct opponents.

LOSING YOUR MARKER

The movement that the forward closest to the ball makes must be preceded with a counter movement to check away from his marker: Short-long, long-short, out-in, in-out. The ball passed to the forward must be played in the opposite direction to the first movement.

The most advanced forward decides for himself when and how to escape his marker. He can do it according to the movement of the other forward (team-mate) or he can wait for the development of the team's attacking move.

POSITIONING

The coach should ask the most advanced forward to position himself in a way that makes the opposition's defensive actions harder (against 2 or 3 centre backs). He must stand behind the opposing centre back who is furthest from the ball, preventing him from watching both the ball and the forward.

This creates 2 possibilities:

1. If the defender drops back so he is able to see both the ball and the forward, the forward has the opportunity to receive a short pass in the space in front of the defence.

2. If the defender decides to maintain the same line and is unable to see the forward, the forward can attack the space in behind and escape his marker with ease.

COMBINATION PLAY

If the 2 forwards are close to each other, combination play between them can be quick. If they play further away from each other, the combinations will be delayed.

This different attacking positioning/shape allows many effective combinations between the forwards when one of them has possession of the ball.

If the forwards are playing as linked players, they must be close and moving around the ball area diagonally; this way, the most advanced forward keeps the opposing defender busy, helping the deeper forward become more difficult to mark.

If the forwards are linked but positioned away from each other, the most advanced forward must be able to both stretch the opposition's defence by dropping back (checking away from marker) and play right up against them (advanced) to play with his team-mate through lay-off passes.

The deeper forward must escape potential markers behind the opposition's midfield line, always trying to position himself with an open body shape towards the opposition's goal. Once the most advanced forward has possession, he is then free in space to combine with him.

2. DEFENSIVE PHASE

STRENGTHS AND WEAKNESSES OF THE 3-5-2 IN THE DEFENSIVE PHASE

STRENGTHS

- Cover central areas of the pitch with many players (3 centre backs, 3 midfielders and 2 forwards).

- Strong defensive central core and numerical superiority against opposing teams with 2 forwards.

- Covering of the weak side is guaranteed by the wing back on that side, who can drop into the defensive line.

WEAKNESSES

- Numerical disadvantage out wide for the wing back against 2 opposing wide players.

- Difficulty in applying aggressive pressing on opposing full backs e.g. Against the 4-4-2 or 4-2-3-1.

- Difficulty in pressing teams that build from the back with 3 centre backs.

- Excessive numerical superiority at the back against teams that play with 1 centre forward, as there is a static situation of 3v1.

- Difficulty in adapting i.e. Changing defensive shape/formation to play against teams that do not play with 2 centre forwards.

2.1 - STRONG CENTRAL DEFENSIVE CORE AND ADAPTING TO DIFFERENT FORMATIONS

STRONG CENTRAL DEFENSIVE CORE AGAINST 2 FORWARDS

Playing with 3 at the back guarantees great density in the centre of the pitch and therefore creates an optimal coverage of the spaces inside this key defensive area.

The defensive stability is provided by a numerical superiority with respect to the number of attackers and the behaviour of the 3 centre backs is most influenced by the movement of those attackers.

Teams that play with 2 forwards or 1 forward and a playmaker (No.10) always have a numerical disadvantage against the 3 centre backs in the 3-5-2 formation. This enables the most important defensive area to be under control, as the players are able to closely mark the attacking players, while also having a spare man always available to provide cover and protect the space in behind.

ADAPTING TO DIFFERENT FORMATIONS

The 3-5-2 formation is well set up to deal with opposing formations with 2 forwards. The difficulties and problems mainly arise against formations that include 3 forwards e.g. 4-3-3.

The solution is generally to switch to a defensive shape with a back 4 to contest the 3 forwards and this will be fully analysed in the next chapter of this book.

In addition, the 3-5-2 formation also encounters a problem defending against teams that play with just 1 forward, but in a different way. There is an excessive numerical superiority in the centre of defence, which creates a numerical disadvantages in other areas of the pitch as a consequence.

In the following chapter, we also analyse this problem and display solutions.

No matter what formation you use, it is very important to be set up with a numerical superiority at the back. To achieve this with the 3-5-2 formation, it is often necessary for 1 or both of the wing backs to drop back into the defensive line, depending on the opponent's system of play.

2.2 - A CENTRE BACK IS ALWAYS ABLE TO PROVIDE COVER ON THE WEAK SIDE

WEAKNESS OF A BACK 4

One of the advantages of playing with 3 centre backs is always having a player available to cover the weak side.

In formations with a back 4, there can be difficulties when an opponent is in possession in a wide position. If the full back moves out aggressively to close the ball carrier down:

- The first centre back takes up a position at the front post to defend the cross.

- The second centre back and the other full back mark the 2 closest players.

- **But what happens if a player moves into the penalty area from the weak side?**

It is not very easy for a central midfielder to read this situation from his position.

STRENGTH OF A BACK 3

However, when playing with a back 3 and the wing back (e.g. **LWB**) moves out aggressively to close the ball carrier down, there are always 3 markers:

- The left centre back (**LCB**) takes up a position at the front post to defend the cross.

- The middle centre back (**CB**) and right centre back (**RCB**) mark the 2 closest players.

- **The right wing back (RWB) is free to mark an opponent who moves into the penalty area from the weak side.**

It should be added that often in these situations teams will have 4 (or more) players positioned in the penalty area, so the defence will need the support of at least 1 of the midfield players. A central midfielder is the most capable of reading the movement of opponents from

central areas, so will be able to perform the necessary defensive duty.

To conclude, I have given an example of a specific way of defending the cross from a wide area: The first centre back takes up a position at the front post and the other players mark the opponents tightly.

However, I feel obliged to point out that there are various solutions including:

- Zone defence with diagonal movement

- Zone defence in pyramid shape

- Man-marking

Despite this, my general example is useful to understand the merit of having the defensive area covered with 5 players (3 centre backs and 2 wing backs form 3-5-2 formation).

2.3 - NUMERICAL DISADVANTAGE IN WIDE AREAS DEFENDED BY 1 WING BACK

A disadvantage in the static set-up of the 3-5-2 system is that the wide areas are overseen by just 1 player (the wing back).

This aspect can lead to difficulties in adapting to play against teams that develop their attacking game in wide areas.

With the 3-5-2 formation, it will often be necessary to move the midfielders into wide areas. In doing so, the difficulties are initially minimal. The middle area of the pitch will come under external pressure with a slight delay, but will manage to close the opposing chain movements. In this case, therefore, the other 2 midfielders will have to tighten in the central area to retain defensive balance.

On one hand, the depth in wide areas is well covered by the wing back. However, on the other hand, if an additional opponent moves into this area to combine, there are no automatic chain movements to defend this.

The coach who decides to adopt this game system must be aware of this "defect" and must try to minimise the problem by making the necessary adjustments.

2.4 - DIFFICULTY IN PERFORMING AGGRESSIVE PRESSING IN THE OPPOSITION HALF

Another structural defect of the 3-5-2 system is related to the difficulty of performing aggressive pressing in the opposition's half.

The difficulties, in this case, are related to the following aspects:

- Pressure on the opposition's full backs.

- Pressure on opposition's deepest central midfielder e.g. Defensive midfielder.

- Structuring of the pressing against teams that build up play from the back with 3 players.

To minimise problems, when structuring the pressing in the opposition's half, the coach will need to both know the characteristics of his players well and be able to accurately assess the

timing of each individual's pressing, to avoid establishing a pressing action with players who are always late on their direct opponents.

With this module, the work in the defensive phase of the attacking and midfield lines is essential.

For this reason, the players in these roles need to be dynamic players with good conditional skills, able to make medium to long pressing runs and cover large areas of the pitch during the defensive phase.

CHAPTER 2

TACTICS AGAINST DIFFERENT FORMATIONS

TACTICS AGAINST DIFFERENT FORMATIONS

In this chapter, we analyse the 3-5-2 system against 6 different formations:

1. **4-4-2**
2. **4-2-3-1**
3. **4-3-3**
4. **4-3-1-2**
5. **3-5-2**
6. **3-4-3**

The goal is to outline the adaptations to be implemented without distorting our game system.

The analysis covers both the attacking phase and the defensive phase.

For the ATTACKING PHASE, we are going to identify the following aspects:

- How to Overcome the First Line of Pressing (Build-up Play from the Back)
- How to Move the Ball in Between the Opposition's Midfield and Defensive Lines
- How to Play in Behind the Opposition's Defensive Line

For the DEFENSIVE PHASE, we will explore the following issues:

- How to Press the Opposition as they Build-up Play
- How to Organise the Defensive Line

1. TACTICS AGAINST THE 4-4-2

I.I - OVERCOMING THE FIRST LINE OF PRESSING (BUILD-UP PLAY FROM THE BACK)

The Wide Centre Back Receives in a Wide Position and Dribbles the Ball Forward

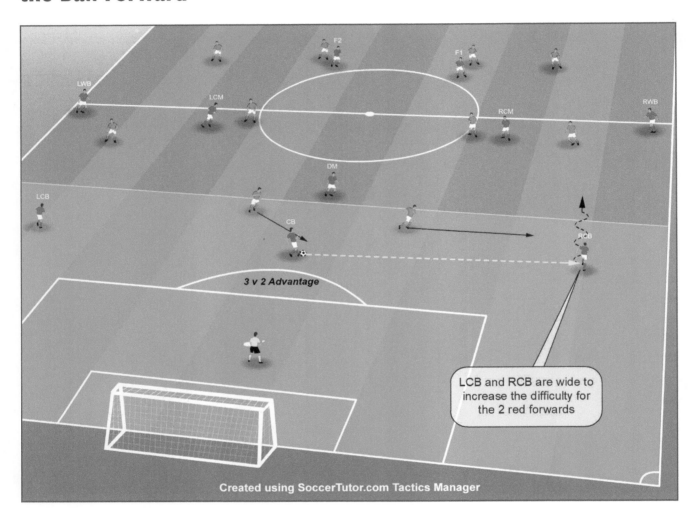

LCB and RCB are wide to increase the difficulty for the 2 red forwards

3 v 2 Advantage

Created using SoccerTutor.com Tactics Manager

When building up play from the back against the 4-4-2, it is important to take advantage of the numerical superiority of 3 defenders against the 2 opposing forwards.

The 3 centre backs stay as open (wide) as possible to increase the difficulty for the 2 forwards to apply pressing and/or mark them.

As a general rule, it should be easy to find one of the wide centre backs in space as the free man.

In this example, the right centre back (**RCB**) receives from the middle centre back (**CB**) in a wide position and dribbles forward.

The blue team using the 3-5-2 formation have successfully overcome the first line of pressing.

I.2 - MOVING THE BALL IN BETWEEN THE OPPOSITION'S MIDFIELD AND DEFENSIVE LINES

A. Wide Centre Back's Options to Play Through the Opposition's Midfield when Pressed by the Opposing Winger

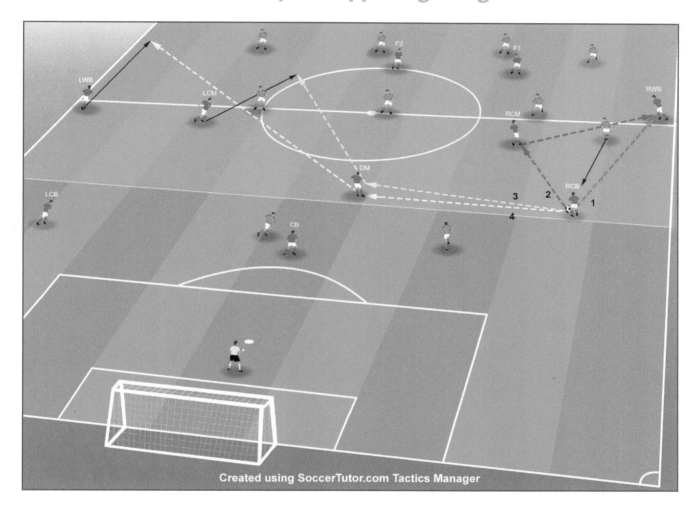

Created using SoccerTutor.com Tactics Manager

Following the right centre back (**RCB**) dribbling forward out of defence (see previous page), his aim is now to move the ball to a team-mate in between the opposition's midfield and defensive lines.

The right centre back (**RCB**) is being closed down by the opposing red team's left winger.

These are the 4 Options for the RCB:

1. Pass directly to the right wing back (**RWB**) in an advanced wide position.

2. Pass to the right wing back (**RWB**) via the right central midfielder (**RCM**).

3. Pass inside to the defensive midfielder (**DM**) in space, who plays a diagonal pass for the forward run of the left central midfielder (**LCM**) in behind the red team's midfield line.

4. Pass inside to the defensive midfielder (**DM**) in space, who uses the space created by **LCM's** forward run to switch the play out wide to the left wing back (**LWB**).

B. Wide Centre Back's Options to Play Through the Opposition's Midfield when Pressed by the Central Midfielder

Created using SoccerTutor.com Tactics Manager

This is a variation of the example on the previous page, with the right centre back (**RCB**) now being closed down by the opposing red team's left central midfielder, instead of the winger.

These are the 4 Options for the RCB:

1. Diagonal pass directly to the right wing back (**RWB**) in an advanced wide position.

2. Forward pass directly to the right central midfielder (**RCM**).

3. Pass to the right central midfielder (**RCM**) via the defensive midfielder (**DM**).

4. Pass to the defensive midfielder (**DM**) in space, who switches the play with a long pass out wide to the advanced left wing back (**LWB**).

NOTE: The choice of the options above mainly depends on how the opposing central midfielder presses and what passing lanes are available.

C. Middle Centre Back's Options to Play Through the Opposition's Midfield when Dribbling Through the Centre

Created using SoccerTutor.com Tactics Manager

In this example, the middle centre back (**CB**) has dribbled out from defence through the centre of the pitch.

These are the **4 Options** for the CB:

1. Diagonal pass to the right wing back (**RWB**), who makes a forward run to receive a pass travelling in between the red winger and central midfielder.

2. Forward pass in between the 2 opposing red central midfielders, directly to the blue right central midfielder (**RCM**).

3. Pass to the right central midfielder (**RCM**) via the defensive midfielder (**DM**).

4. Switch play with a long aerial pass out wide to the left wing back (**LWB**), who makes a forward run to receive.

NOTE: The choice of the options above mainly depends on how the opposing player presses and what passing lanes are available.

I.3 - PLAYING IN BEHIND THE OPPOSITION'S DEFENSIVE LINE

A. The Wing Back Decides Whether to Play in Behind or Pass Inside Based on the Opposition's Pressing

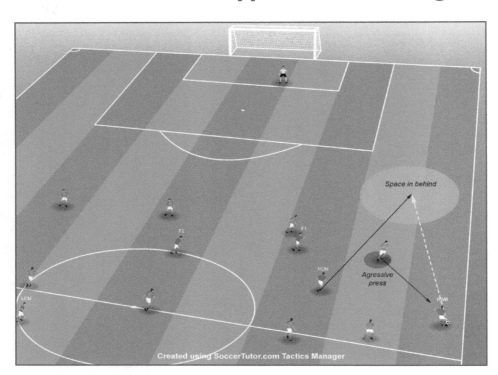

When the wing back is in possession, he must make decisions based on the pressing of the opponents.

In this first example, the right wing back (**RWB**) is pressed aggressively by the opposing left back.

In this situation, the **RWB** must pass into the space created.

The right central midfielder (**RCM**) makes a forward run to receive in behind.

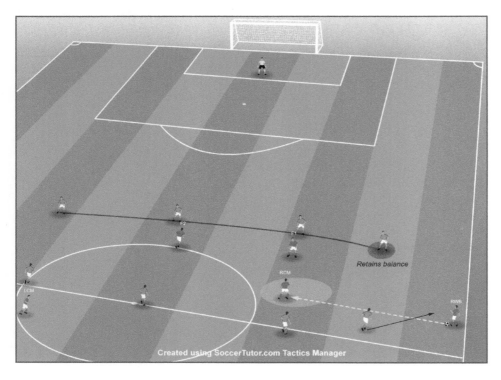

In this variation, the opposing left back retains his balanced position within the back 4, so there is no space in behind him to exploit.

The blue **RWB** is pressed by the red left winger this time, so simply passes inside for the right central midfielder (**RCM**) to receive in between the lines.

See the following page for **RCM's** options...

B. Central Midfielder's Options to Play in Behind the Defensive Line After Receiving Between the Lines

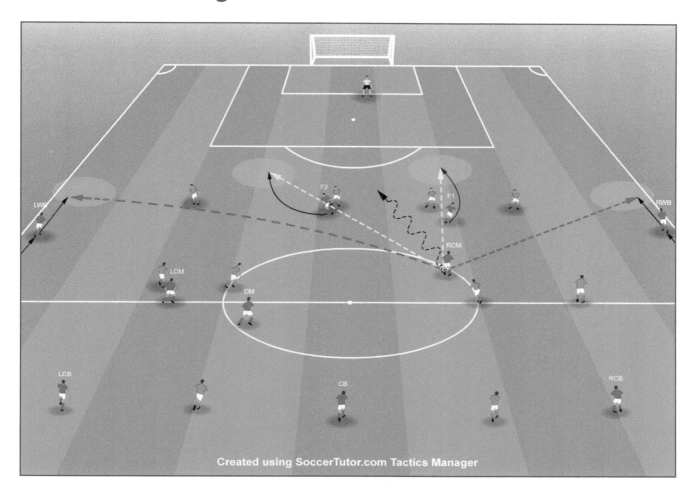

Created using SoccerTutor.com Tactics Manager

Following the right central midfielder (**RCM**) receiving between the lines (see previous page), his aim is now to move the ball to a team-mate in behind the opposition's defensive line.

These are the <u>3 Options</u> for the RCM:

1. If the 2 opposing centre backs are close together and the 2 full backs are open, space is available for either forward to run into and receive in behind (see yellow arrows).

2. If the 2 centre backs stay fairly wide and cover the runs of the 2 forwards, the right central midfielder (**RCM**) can continue to dribble forward and commit the defenders in a 3v2 or 5v4 situation.

3. If the whole of the red team's back 4 is compact and narrow, then there is space to be exploited out wide by passing to either wing back, who can make advanced runs as shown (see blue arrows).

1.4 - PRESSING AND DEFENSIVE ORGANISATION

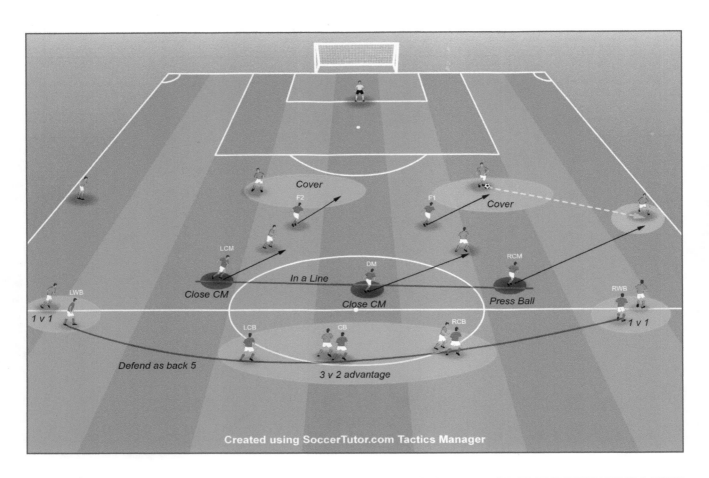

HOW TO PRESS THE OPPOSITION (4-4-2) AS THEY BUILD-UP PLAY?

- The 3 midfielders (**DM**, **LCM** & **RCM**) must immediately position themselves in a line.

- With the ball played to the red full back, the 2 blue forwards (**F1** & **F2**) move to cover the 2 red centre backs.

- The right central midfielder (**RCM**) moves across to press the new ball carrier.

- The defensive midfielder (**DM**) and the left central midfielder (**LCM**) move to close down the opposing red central midfielders.

HOW TO ORGANISE THE DEFENSIVE LINE?

- The defensive line is formed of 5 players, including the 2 wing backs.

- The 3 centre backs (**LCB**, **CB** & **RCB**) have a 3 v 2 numerical superiority against the 2 red forwards.

- The wing backs (**LWB** & **RWB**) defend with individual duels (1 v 1) against the 2 red wingers.

2. TACTICS AGAINST THE 4-2-3-1

2.1 - OVERCOMING THE FIRST LINE OF PRESSING (BUILD-UP PLAY FROM THE BACK)

A. The Ball is Moved Easily Between the 3 Centre Backs Against the 1 Opposing Forward

3 v 1 Advantage

LCB and RCB are distant enough to make it difficult for the forward to press

Created using SoccerTutor.com Tactics Manager

When building up play from the back against the 4-2-3-1, the team has a 3v1 numerical superiority against the 1 forward.

The 3 centre backs are distant from each other (but not too much) so it's difficult for the forward to apply pressing and/or mark them.

If the forward tries to press one of the wide centre backs, they can just easily and calmly move the ball to the other wide centre back, as shown in the diagram example above.

In this example, the left centre back (**LCB**) is put under pressure from the 1 red forward after the middle centre back's (**CB**) pass. He passes to the right centre back (**RCB**), who can dribble forward freely.

The blue team using the 3-5-2 formation have successfully overcome the first line of pressing.

B. Tactical Solution to Build-up Play when the Opposition Wingers Move Up to Press the Wide Centre Backs

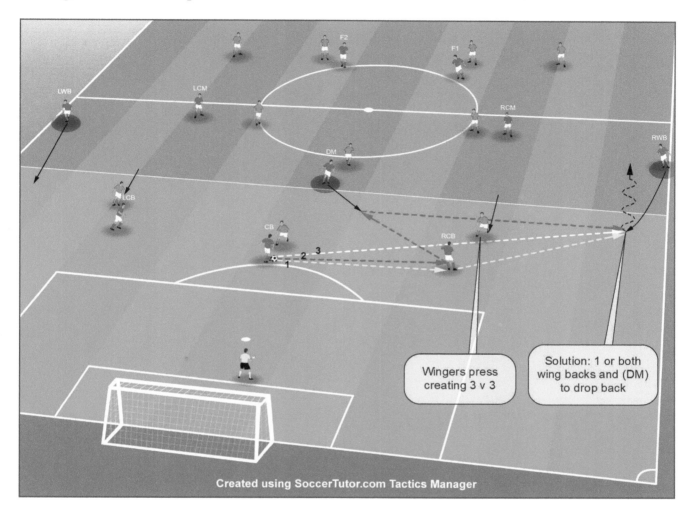

Wingers press creating 3 v 3

Solution: 1 or both wing backs and (DM) to drop back

Created using SoccerTutor.com Tactics Manager

If the opposing team (using the 4-2-3-1) decide to move their wingers into advanced positions to apply 3 v 3 pressing against the 3 centre backs, the blue team need to adapt quickly to recreate a numerical superiority at the back to build-up play.

The tactical solution is for 1 or both wing backs and the defensive midfielder (**DM**) to drop back closer to the defence.

In this example, the middle centre back (**CB**) has possession and the left centre back (**LCB**) is closely marked.

These are the **3 Options** for the blue team to successfully overcome the first line of pressing from the 3 red attackers:

1. The right wing back (**RWB**) drops back. The middle centre back (**CB**) passes to the right centre back (**RCB**), who then passes out wide to the right wing back (**RWB**).

2. The defensive midfielder (**DM**) drops back. The middle centre back (**CB**) passes to the right centre back (**RCB**), who passes to the **DM**. The **DM** then passes out wide to the right wing back (**RWB**).

3. If the opposing winger is closely marking the right centre back (**RCB**) and there is a clear passing lane, the middle centre back (**CB**) passes directly to the right wing back (**RWB**).

2.2 - MOVING THE BALL IN BETWEEN THE OPPOSITION'S MIDFIELD AND DEFENSIVE LINES

A. Wide Centre Back's Options to Play Through the Opposition's Midfield when Pressed by the Opposing Winger

Created using SoccerTutor.com Tactics Manager

The right centre back (**RCB**) is being closed down by the opposing red team's left winger and the aim is to move the ball to a team-mate in between the opposition's midfield and defensive lines.

These are the 3 Options for the RCB:

1. Pass directly to the right wing back (**RWB**).

2. Pass to the right wing back (**RWB**) via the right central midfielder (**RCM**).

3. The defensive midfielder (**DM**) moves forward to create space and drag his marker (red No.10) away. The left central midfielder (**LCM**) drops back into the space created to receive from the right centre back (**RCB**). He then plays the ball out wide to the advanced left wing back (**LWB**), who has made a forward run.

NOTE: The choice of the options above mainly depends on how the opposing winger presses and what passing lanes are available.

B. Wide Centre Back's Options to Play Through the Opposition's Midfield when Pressed by the Central Midfielder

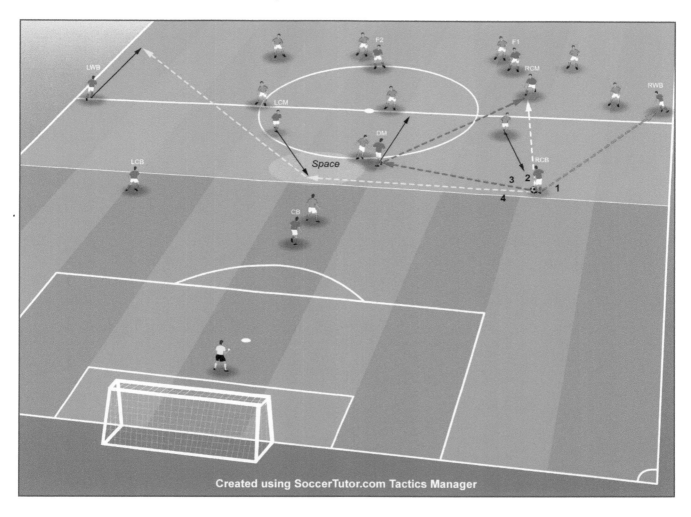

Created using SoccerTutor.com Tactics Manager

This is a variation of the example on the previous page, with the right centre back (**RCB**) now being closed down by the opposing red team's central midfielder, instead of the winger.

These are the 4 Options for the RCB:

1. Pass directly to the right wing back (**RWB**).

2. Pass directly to the right central midfielder (**RCM**), if there is an available passing lane.

3. Pass to the right central midfielder (**RCM**) via the defensive midfielder (**DM**).

4. The defensive midfielder (**DM**) moves forward to create space and drag his marker (red No.10) away. The left central midfielder (**LCM**) drops back into the space created to receive from the right centre back (**RCB**). He then plays the ball out wide to the advanced left wing back (**LWB**), who has made a forward run.

NOTE: The choice of the options above mainly depends on how the opposing central midfielder presses and what passing lanes are available.

C. The Wing Back's Options to Play Through the Opposition's Midfield when Dribbling Forward

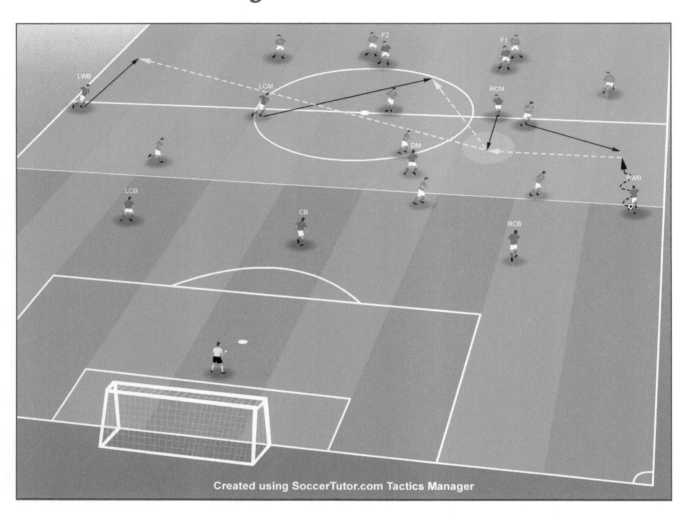

Created using SoccerTutor.com Tactics Manager

On page 47, we show how the wing back drops back to help build-up play from the back when the opposition press the 3 centre backs with 3 attackers.

This tactical example follows on from there, with the wing back in possession dribbling forward and aiming to move the ball to a team-mate in between the opposition's midfield and defensive lines.

The right wing back (**RWB**) is pressed by a central midfielder, so has limited time, space and options to play.

In this example, the right central midfielder (**RCM**) drops back to create a simple passing option inside and the **RWB** passes him the ball.

The aim is to then move the ball to a team-mate in between the opposition's midfield lines.

These are the 2 Options for the RCM:

1. Diagonal pass for the diagonal run of the left central midfielder (**LCM**).

2. Use the movement of the left central midfielder (**LCM**) to easily pass out wide (switch play) to the left wing back (**LWB**) in an advanced position on the flank.

2.3 - PLAYING IN BEHIND THE OPPOSITION'S DEFENSIVE LINE

A. The Wing Back Decides Whether to Play in Behind or Pass Inside Based on the Opposition's Pressing

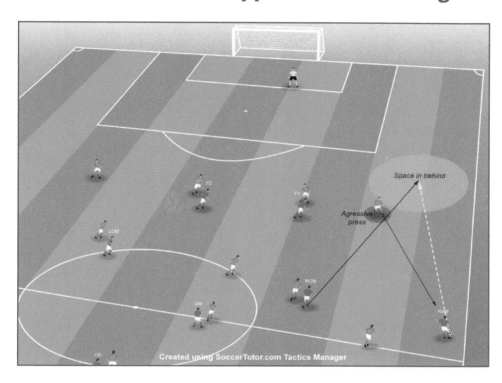

When the wing back is in possession, he must make decisions based on the pressing of the opponents.

In this first example, the right wing back (**RWB**) is pressed aggressively by the opposing left back.

In this situation, the **RWB** must pass into the space created.

The right central midfielder (**RCM**) makes a forward run to receive in behind.

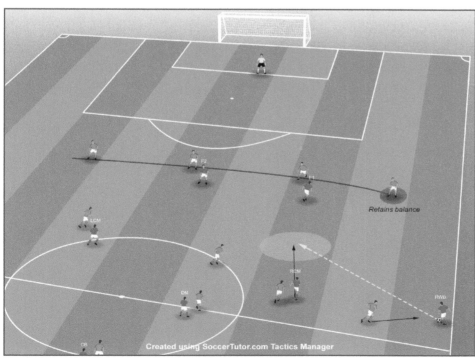

In this variation, the opposing left back retains his balanced position within the back 4, so there is no space in behind him to exploit.

The blue right wing back (**RWB**) is pressed by the red left winger this time, so instead passes in front of the right central midfielder (**RCM**) to receive (on the run) in between the lines.

See the following page for **RCM's** options...

B. Central Midfielder's Options to Play in Behind the Defensive Line After Receiving Between the Lines

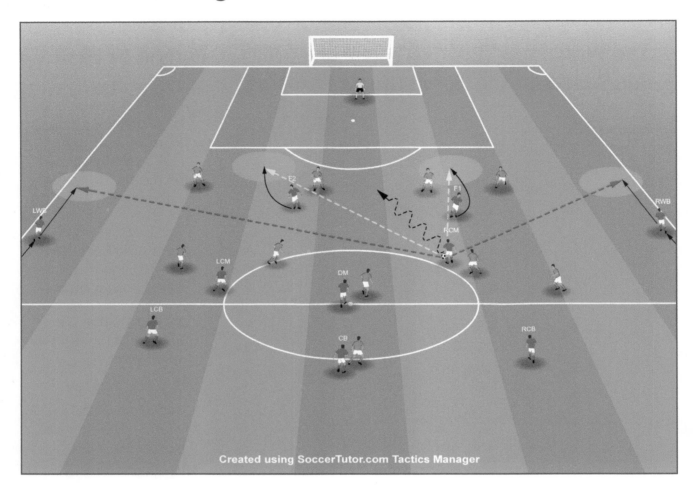

Created using SoccerTutor.com Tactics Manager

Following the right central midfielder (**RCM**) receiving between the lines (see previous page), his aim is now to move the ball to a team-mate in behind the opposition's defensive line.

These are the <u>3 Options</u> for the RCM:

1. If the 2 opposing centre backs are close together and the 2 full backs are open, space is available for either forward to run into and receive in behind (see yellow arrows).

2. If the 2 centre backs stay fairly wide and cover the runs of the 2 forwards, the right central midfielder (**RCM**) can continue to dribble forward and commit the defenders in a 3v2 or 5v4 situation.

3. If the whole of the red team's back 4 is compact and narrow, then there is space to be exploited out wide by passing to either wing back, who can make advanced runs as shown (see blue arrows).

2.4 - PRESSING AND DEFENSIVE ORGANISATION

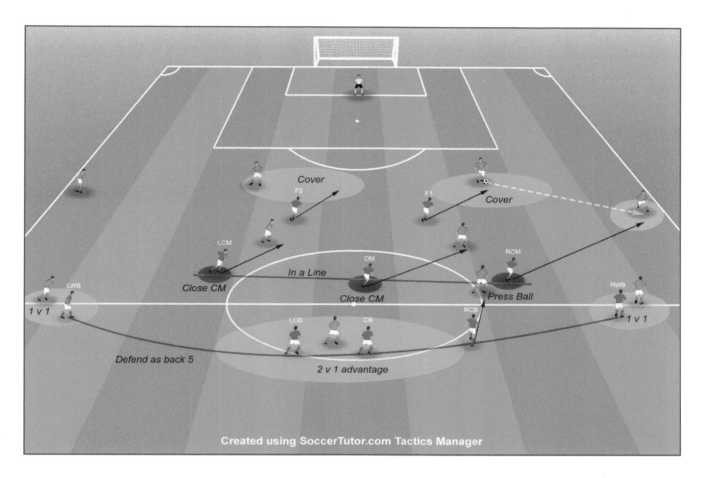

Created using SoccerTutor.com Tactics Manager

HOW TO PRESS THE OPPOSITION (4-2-3-1) AS THEY BUILD-UP PLAY?

- The 3 midfielders (**DM**, **LCM** & **RCM**) must immediately position themselves in a line.

- With the ball played to the red full back, the 2 blue forwards (**F1** & **F2**) move to cover the 2 red centre backs.

- The right central midfielder (**RCM**) moves across to press the new ball carrier.

- The defensive midfielder (**DM**) and the left central midfielder (**LCM**) move to close down the opposing red central midfielders.

- As the right central midfielder (**RCM**) leaves his position, the right centre back (**RCB**) moves forward to mark the red No.10.

HOW TO ORGANISE THE DEFENSIVE LINE?

- Initially (before **RCB** moves forward), the defensive line is formed of 5 players including the 2 wing backs. This changes to a back 4 after he moves to mark the red No.10.

- The 2 centre backs (**LCB** & **CB**) have a 2 v 1 numerical superiority against the 1 red forward.

- The wing backs (**LWB** & **RWB**) defend with individual duels (1 v 1) against the 2 red wingers.

3. TACTICS AGAINST THE 4-3-3

3.1 - OVERCOMING THE FIRST LINE OF PRESSING (BUILD-UP PLAY FROM THE BACK)

A. The Ball is Moved Easily Between the 3 Centre Backs Against the 1 Opposing Forward

When building up play from the back against the 4-3-3, the team has a 3v1 numerical superiority against the 1 forward.

The 3 centre backs are distant from each other (but not too much) so it's difficult for the forward to apply pressing and/or mark them.

Usually in this situation, a wide centre back is able to receive in space and exploit the situation to move the team forward and overcome the first line of pressing.

In this example, the middle centre back (**CB**) is put under pressure by the red forward and passes to the right centre back (**RCB**).

These are the 2 Options for the RCB:

1. If the red forward is unable to press the **RCB**, he can dribble the ball forward freely.

2. If the red forward is able to apply pressure, the **RCB** can easily pass to the defensive midfielder (**DM**), who is free in the centre.

B. Tactical Solution when the Opposition Wingers Move Up to Press: Wing Backs and DM Drop Back

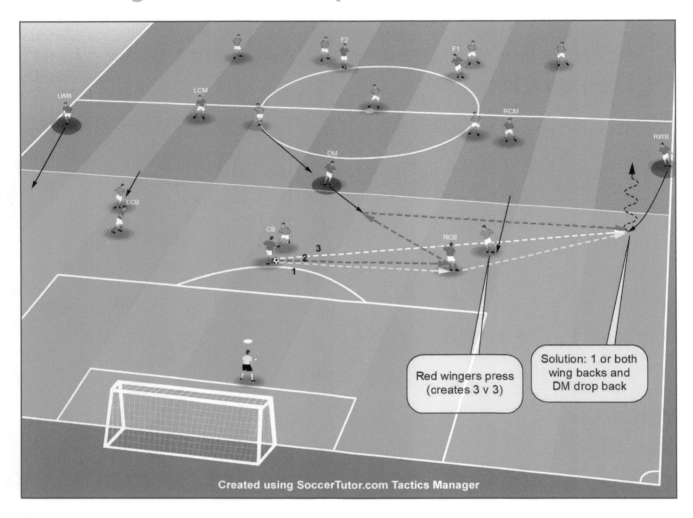

Red wingers press
(creates 3 v 3)

Solution: 1 or both
wing backs and
DM drop back

Created using SoccerTutor.com Tactics Manager

If the opposing team decide to move their wingers into advanced positions to apply 3 v 3 pressing against the 3 centre backs, the blue team need to adapt quickly to recreate a numerical superiority at the back and build-up play.

The tactical solution is for 1 or both wing backs and the defensive midfielder (**DM**) to drop back closer to the defence.

In this example, the middle centre back (**CB**) has possession and the left centre back (**LCB**) is closely marked.

These are the **3 Options** for the blue team to successfully overcome the first line of pressing from the 3 red attackers:

1. The right wing back (**RWB**) drops back. The middle centre back (**CB**) passes to the right centre back (**RCB**), who then passes out wide to the right wing back (**RWB**).

2. The defensive midfielder (**DM**) drops back. The middle centre back (**CB**) passes to the right centre back (**RCB**), who passes to the defensive midfielder (**DM**). The **DM** then passes out wide to the right wing back (**RWB**).

3. If the opposing winger is closely marking the right centre back (**RCB**) and there is a clear passing lane, the middle centre back (**CB**) passes directly to the right wing back (**RWB**).

C. Tactical Solution when the Opposition Wingers Move Up to Press: Defensive Midfielder Receives

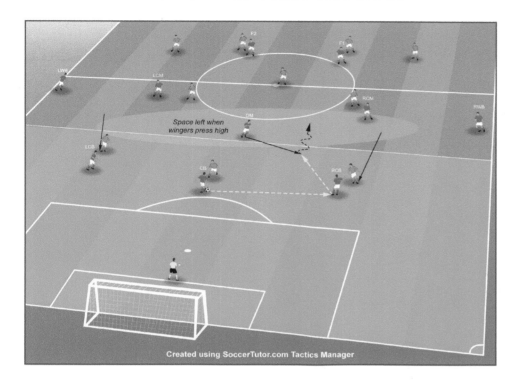

When the opposing team are playing with the 4-3-3 formation and press high with both wingers, they often leave a large space in between their attacking and midfield lines.

In this example, the defensive midfielder (**DM**) is able to receive a simple pass in the middle and dribble forward into the space.

D. Tactical Solution when the Opposition Wingers Move Up to Press: Defensive Midfielder Drops Back into Defensive Line

In this variation, the wide centre backs (**LCB** & **RCB**) push very wide to drag their markers (red wingers) away and create more space in the centre of the pitch.

The defensive midfielder (**DM**) is able to drop back into the defensive line to create a 2v1 numerical advantage in the centre, receive from the middle centre back (**CB**) and dribble forward into space.

3.2 - MOVING THE BALL IN BETWEEN THE OPPOSITION'S MIDFIELD AND DEFENSIVE LINES

A. Wide Centre Back's Options to Play Through the Opposition's Midfield when Pressed by the Opposing Winger

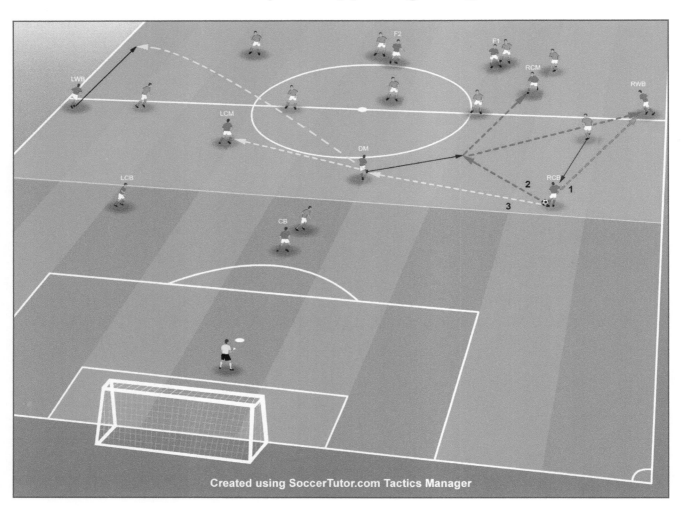

Created using SoccerTutor.com Tactics Manager

The right centre back (**RCB**) is being closed down by the opposing red team's left winger and the aim is to move the ball to a team-mate in between the opposition's midfield and defensive lines.

These are the <u>3 Options</u> for the RCB:

1. Pass directly to the right wing back (**RWB**).

2. Pass to the right wing back (**RWB**) or right central midfielder (**RCM**) via the defensive midfielder (**DM**), who moves across.

3. Pass inside to the defensive midfielder (**DM**) in space, who either passes short to the left central midfielder (**LCM**) or switches the play out wide to the left wing back (**LWB**) in an advanced position on the flank.

NOTE: The choice of the options above mainly depends on how the opposing winger presses and what passing lanes are available.

B. Wide Centre Back's Options to Play Through the Opposition's Midfield when Pressed by the Central Midfielder

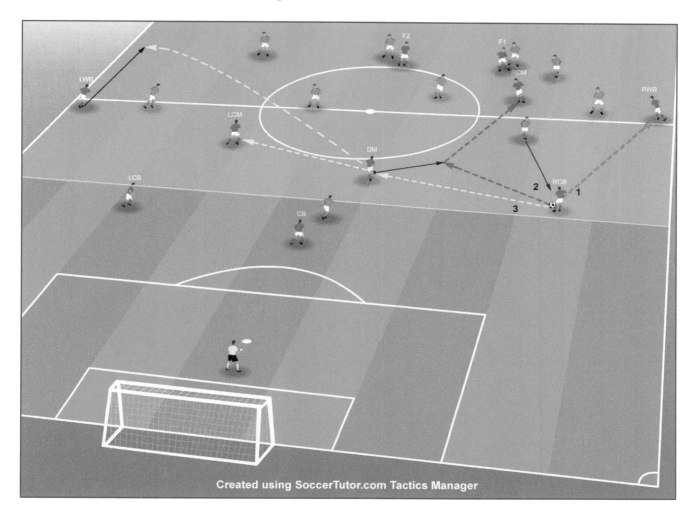

This is a variation of the example on the previous page, with the right centre back (**RCB**) now being closed down by the opposing red team's central midfielder, instead of the winger.

These are the <u>3 Options</u> for the RCB:

1. Pass directly to the right wing back (**RWB**).

2. Pass to the right central midfielder (**RCM**) via the defensive midfielder (**DM**), who moves across.

3. Pass inside to the defensive midfielder (**DM**) in space, who either passes short to the left central midfielder (**LCM**) or switches the play out wide to the left wing back (**LWB**) in an advanced position on the flank.

NOTE: The choice of the options above mainly depends on how the opposing central midfielder presses and what passing lanes are available.

C. The Wing Back's Options to Play Through the Opposition's Midfield when Dribbling Forward

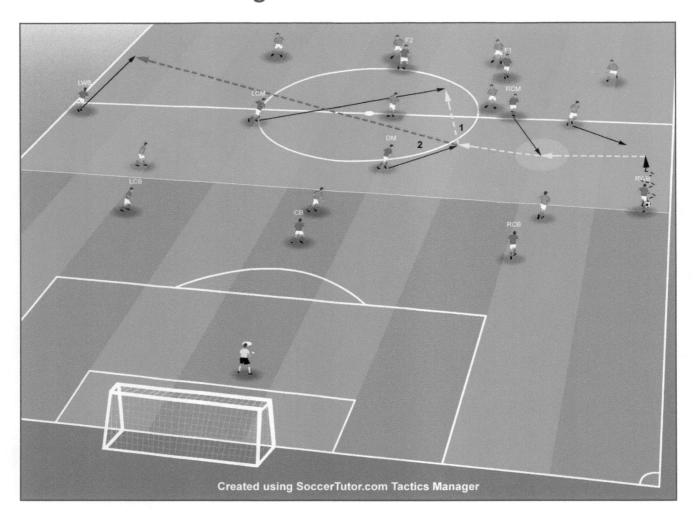

This tactical example shows the wing back in a deep position, dribbling forward and aiming to move the ball to a team-mate in between the opposition's midfield and defensive lines.

The right wing back (**RWB**) is pressed by the red left winger, so has limited time, space and options to play.

In this example, the right central midfielder (**RCM**) drops back to create a simple passing option inside and the right wing back (**RWB**) passes him the ball.

The right central midfielder (**RCM**) passes inside again to the defensive midfielder (**DM**), who moves across to receive and then play to a team-mate in between the lines.

These are the 2 Options for the DM:

1. Diagonal pass for the diagonal run of the left central midfielder (**LCM**).

2. Pass out wide (switch play) to the left wing back (**LWB**) in an advanced position on the flank.

D. Defensive Midfielder's Options to Play Through the Opposition's Midfield when Dribbling Through the Centre

Following the opposition's front 3 applying a high press against the 3 blue centre backs, the defensive midfielder (**DM**) is able to easily receive in the middle of the pitch (see page 57).

The defensive midfielder's (**DM**) aim is to move the ball to a team-mate in between the opposition's midfield and defensive lines.

These are the 4 Options for the DM:

1. Pass to the right wing back (**RWB**), who makes a forward run into an advanced wide position.

2. Forward pass in between the 2 opposing red central midfielders, directly to the blue right central midfielder (**RCM**).

3. Pass to the right central midfielder (**RCM**) via the left central midfielder (**LCM**), who drops back and across.

4. Switch play with a long pass out wide to the left wing back (**LWB**), who makes a forward run to receive.

NOTE: The choice of the options above mainly depends on how the opposing central midfielder presses and what passing lanes are available.

3.3 - PLAYING IN BEHIND THE OPPOSITION'S DEFENSIVE LINE

A. The Wing Back Decides Whether to Play in Behind or Pass Inside Based on the Opposition's Pressing

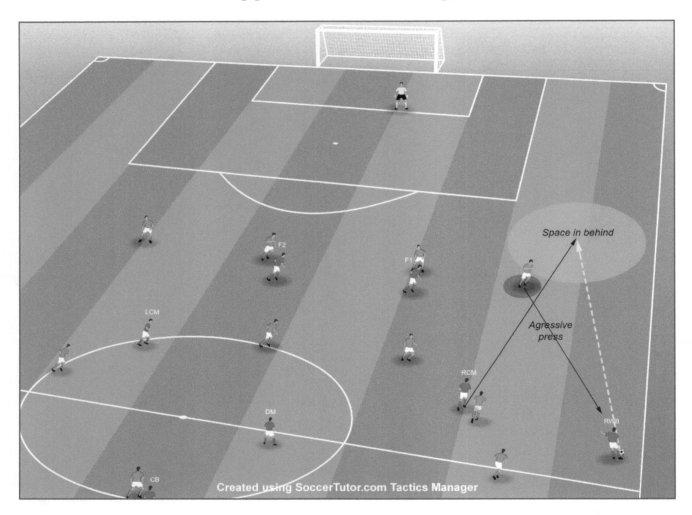

When the wing back is in possession, he must make decisions based on the pressing of the opponents.

In this first example, the right wing back (**RWB**) is pressed aggressively by the opposing left back.

In this situation, the right wing back (**RWB**) must pass into the space created.

The right central midfielder (**RCM**) makes a forward run to receive in behind.

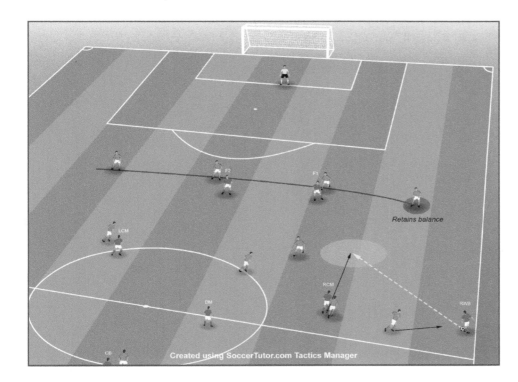

In this variation, the opposing left back retains his balanced position within the back 4, so there is no space in behind him to exploit.

The blue right wing back (**RWB**) is pressed by the red left winger this time, so he instead passes in front of the right central midfielder (**RCM**) to receive on the run in between the lines.

See the next page for **RCM's** options...

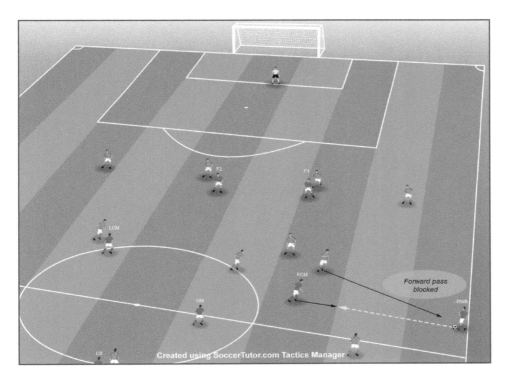

In this variation, the opposing left winger is ahead of the ball and presses in a way that prevents a forward pass.

The blue right wing back (**RWB**) has little time, space or options, therefore passes to the right central midfielder (**RCM**) behind the opposition's midfield line to simply maintain possession for his team.

B. Central Midfielder's Options to Play in Behind the Defensive Line After Receiving Between the Lines

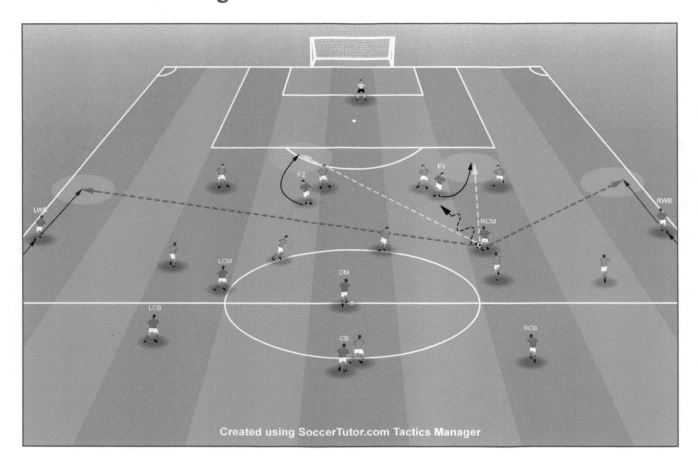

Created using SoccerTutor.com Tactics Manager

Following the right central midfielder (**RCM**) receiving between the lines, his aim is now to move the ball to a team-mate in behind the opposition's defensive line.

These are the 3 Options for the RCM:

1. If the 2 opposing centre backs are close together and the 2 full backs are open, space is available for either forward to run into and receive in behind (see yellow arrows).

2. If the 2 centre backs stay fairly wide and cover the runs of the 2 forwards, the right central midfielder (**RCM**) can continue to dribble forward and commit the defenders in a 3v2 or 5v4 situation.

3. If the whole of the red team's back 4 is compact and narrow, then there is space to be exploited out wide by passing to either wing back (**LWB** or **RWB**), who can make advanced runs as shown (see blue arrows).

3.4 - PRESSING AND DEFENSIVE ORGANISATION IN A 4-4-2 OR 4-4-1-1 SHAPE

Against the 4-3-3 formation, the 3 midfielders must all be positioned in a line together and the focus is on preventing the opposing defensive midfielder from receiving the ball in the centre of the pitch.

When the opposition build-up play from the back, the aim is to force play out wide towards their full backs and then apply pressing. The following pages detail the different tactical solutions for the defensive phase.

A. Pressing the Centre Back Dribbling Forward with a 4-4-2 Defensive Shape

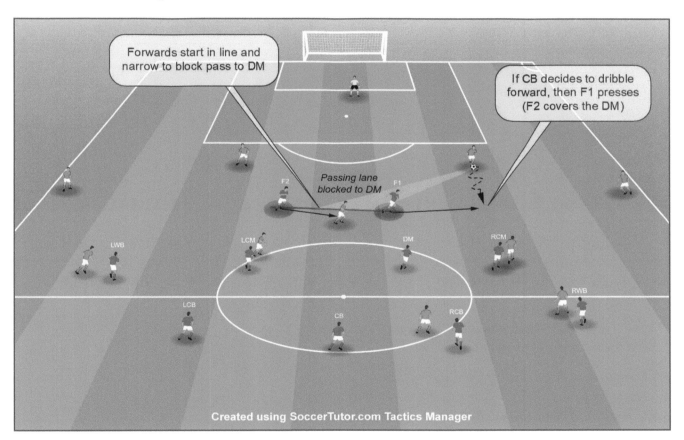

TTo counteract the 4-4-2 formation, the blues change their defensive shape to 4-4-2.

The 2 forwards (**F1** & **F2**) are in line with each other and block the passing lane towards the red defensive midfielder.

This decision allows the red left centre back to dribble the ball forward.

When the red centre back moves forward, the closest blue forward (**F1**) moves to press the ball and the other forward (**F2**) shifts across at the same time to mark the opposing defensive midfielder.

B. Pressing the Centre Back Dribbling Forward with a 4-4-1-1 Defensive Shape

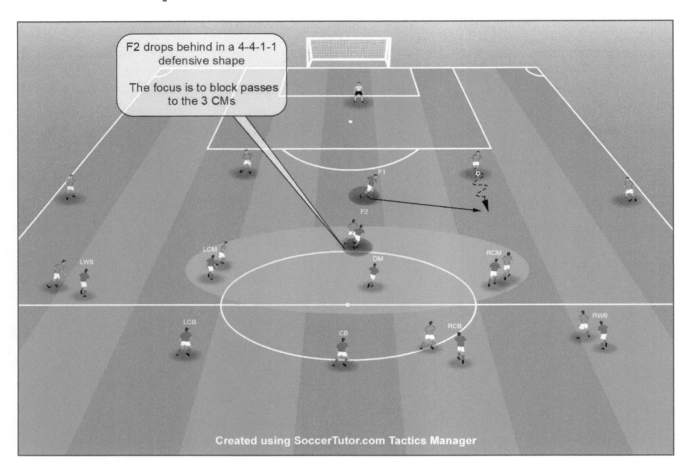

In this second example, the 2 forwards are no longer in line with each other and instead **F2** is behind **F1** as part of the blue team's 4-4-1-1 defensive shape.

The blue forwards again allow the red left centre back to dribble the ball forward.

When the red centre back moves forward, the closest blue forward (**F1**) moves to press the ball again and the other (**F2**) stays in his position to mark the red defensive midfielder.

The main focus for the blue team is to prevent their opponents from passing to a team-mate in a central area. The 3 red central midfielders are all marked tightly.

C. The Central Midfielder Moves to Press the Full Back and Other Players Shift to Mark Potential Receivers

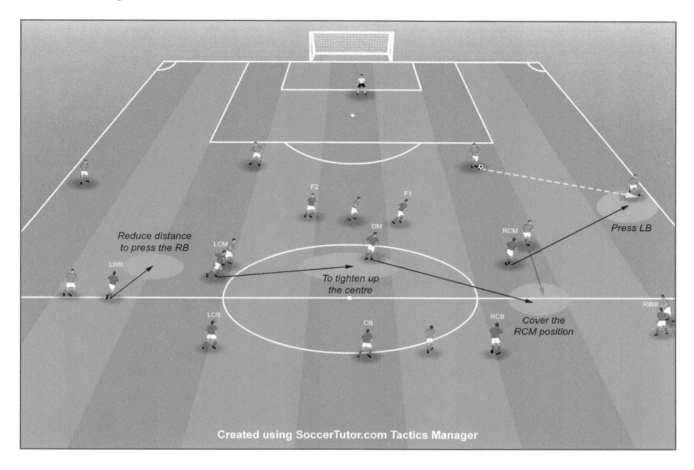

NOTE: This example is shown with the 2 forwards in a horizontal line within the 4-4-2 defensive shape, but the same conditions apply if changed to 1 forward behind the other in the 4-4-1-1 defensive shape.

In this tactical situation, the red centre back does not dribble forward. Instead, he passes out wide to the left back who is free with available time and space.

There are **2 Options** for who closes down the red right back:

1. The right central midfielder (**RCM**).
2. The right wing back (**RWB**).

For this example, we show what happens with option 1. The right central midfielder (**RCM**) moves to close down the red left back and this creates the following chain reaction of the other

players to protect the centre of the pitch:

1. The defensive midfielder's (**DM**) movement completely depends on the movement of the red opponents in midfield. In this example, the **DM** shifts across and back to cover the right central midfielder's (**RCM**) position and mark the opposing red left central midfielder, who has made a forward run.

2. The left central midfielder (**LCM**) moves inside to tighten the centre of the pitch.

3. The left wing back (**LWB**) pushes forward to reduce the distance he has to the red right back. Should the ball reach the opposing red right back, the **LWB** would be the one to press him.

D. The Central Midfielder Moves to Press the Full Back and the Opposing Central Midfielder and Winger Switch Positions

NOTE: The left wing back is deeper here (in back 4) and the right wing back is in a more advanced position and this example shows a different reaction from the opposing left central midfielder and left winger, as they switch positions. The red left winger moves inside into the centre and the left central midfielder moves out wide.

This changing situation requires a different reaction from the blue defending team.

The right central midfielder (**RCM**) has again moved to close down the red left back and this creates the following chain reaction of the other players to protect the centre of the pitch:

1. The defensive midfielder (**DM**) shifts across to cover the right central midfielder's (**RCM**)

position and mark the opposing red left winger, who has moved inside off the flank.

2. The right wing back (**RWB**) moves forward to mark the red left central midfielder, who has moved into a wide position.

3. The left central midfielder (**LCM**) moves inside to tighten the centre of the pitch.

4. The left wing back (**LWB**) moves into the midfield line to reduce the distance he has to the red right back. Should the ball reach the opposing red right back, the **LWB** would be the one to press him.

E. One Wing Back Moves to Press the Full Back and the Other Wing Back Drops Back to Create a Back 4

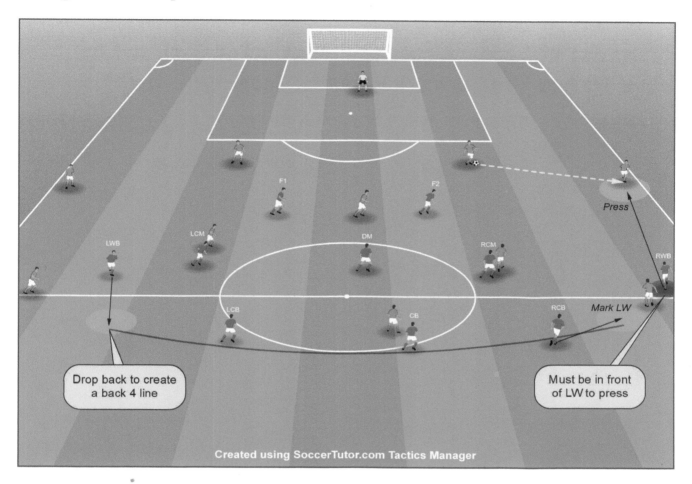

If the pressing of the opposing full back is to be done by a wing back, he must first be positioned in front of the opposing winger.

The central midfielder on that side (**RCM**) or the wide centre back (**RCB**) will mark the opposing winger and the other players will react to mark the other opponents in the centre of the pitch.

As one wing back (**RWB**) moves forward to close down the opposing full back, the other wing back (**LWB**) drops back to create a back 4 line. Should the ball reach the opposing red right back, the left central midfielder (**LCM**) would be the one to press him.

- **Advantage of Pressing with the Central Midfielder** = Higher pressing.

- **Disadvantage of Pressing with the Central Midfielder** = The opposing central midfielder can easily read the movement and there is a difficulty in defending a long pass towards the opposite winger.

- **Advantage of Pressing with the Wing Back** = Keep more numbers in the central area to remain solid, while still protecting the wide areas.

- **Disadvantage of Pressing with the Wing Back** = More delayed pressing and the initial position of the wing back in front of the opposing winger risks a potential 3v3 situation from a long pass (direct attack).

3.5 - PRESSING AND DEFENSIVE ORGANISATION IN A 5-3-2 SHAPE

A. Central Midfielder Moves to Press the Full Back and the Other Players Shift to Mark Potential Receivers

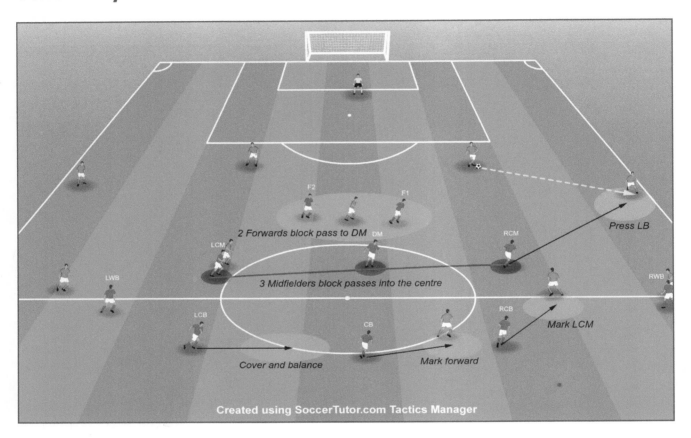

Against the 4-3-3, the 3 midfielders must all be positioned in a line together and the focus is on preventing the opposition from moving the ball into the centre of the pitch:

1. The 2 blue forwards block the passing lanes towards the opposing defensive midfielder.

2. The 3 blue midfielders make sure to block the passing lanes into the centre or apply tight marking to the opposing central midfielders.

In this example, the opposing full back has received in a wide position. When defending in a 3-5-2 shape, the coach should be focussed on the combined movement of the wide centre back (**RCB**), central midfielder (**RCM**) and wing

back (**RWB**) on that side of the pitch. These 3 players have to deal with marking the opposing red central midfielder, winger and forward.

The right central midfielder (**RCM**) moves forward to press the opposing left back. The right wing back's (**RWB**) defensive reaction is determined by the opponents.

In this first example, the opposing red left winger doesn't move and is closely marked by the blue right wing back (**RWB**). Therefore, the right centre back (**RCB**) moves forward to mark the red left central midfielder and the blue **CB** and **LCB** shift across at the same time.

B. Central Midfielder Moves to Press the Full Back and the Opposing Central Midfielder and Winger Switch Positions

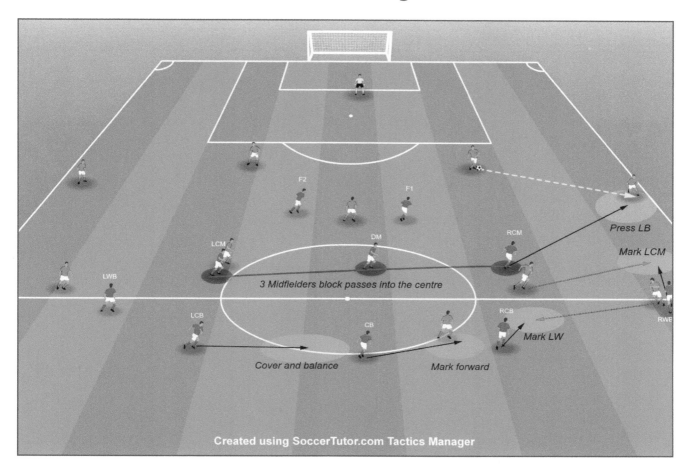

NOTE: This example shows a different reaction from the opposing left central midfielder and left winger, as they switch positions. The red left winger moves inside off the flank into the centre and the left central midfielder moves out wide.

This changing situation requires a different reaction from the blue defending team.

The right central midfielder (**RCM**) has again moved to close down the red left back and this creates the following chain reaction to mark the red central midfielder, winger and forward:

1. The right centre back (**RCB**) moves forward to mark the opposing red left winger, who has moved inside off the flank.

2. The right wing back (**RWB**) moves forward to mark the red left central midfielder, who has moved into a wide position.

3. The middle centre back (**CB**) moves across to mark the opposing red forward.

4. The left centre back (**LCB**) shifts across as part of the chain reaction to maintain balance in the defensive line.

C. Wing Back Moves to Press the Full Back and the Opposing Midfielder and Winger Make Opposite Vertical Movements

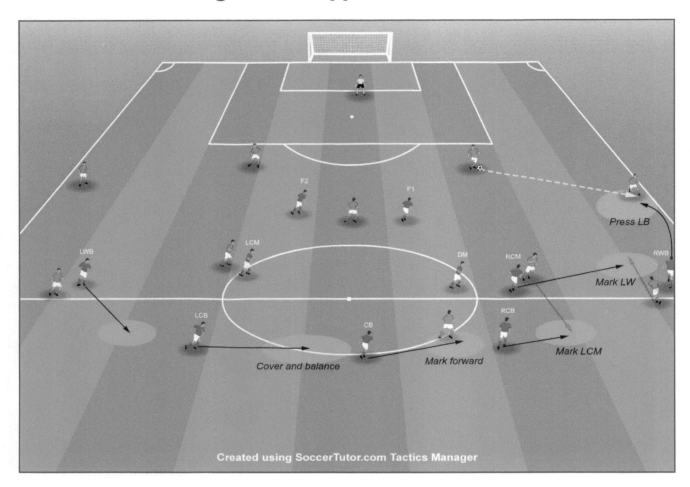

If the pressing of the opposing full back is to be done by the wing back, the coach must make sure that the wing back presses in a way that blocks the pass up the line towards the opposing winger. The wing back wants to press with the correct body shape to force the ball carrier to play inside, where the team have plenty of players and defensive stability.

The defensive reaction of the right central midfielder (**RCM**) and the right centre back (**RCB**) depends on the movements of the opposing red left central midfielder and left winger.

The right wing back (**RWB**) has moved forward to close down the red left back and this creates the following chain reaction to mark the red central midfielder, winger and forward:

1. The right central midfielder (**RCM**) moves across to mark the opposing left winger, who has dropped back.

2. The right centre back (**RCB**) moves across to mark the opposing red left central midfielder, who makes an opposite forward movement.

3. The middle centre back (**CB**) moves across to mark the opposing red forward.

4. The left centre back (**LCB**) shifts across as part of the chain reaction, providing cover and balance.

5. The left wing back (**LWB**) drops back into the defensive line to create balance and a numerical superiority in defence.

D. Wing Back Moves to Press the Full Back and the Opposing Central Midfielder Moves to Receive Short

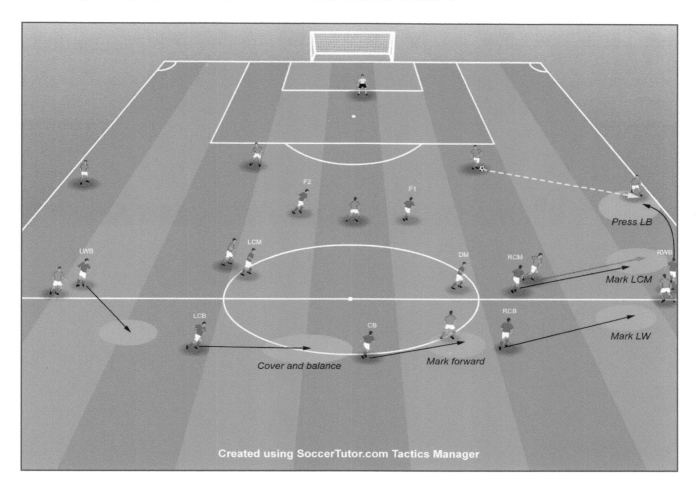

Created using SoccerTutor.com Tactics Manager

In this example, the opposing red left winger doesn't move and the red left central midfielder drops back to try and receive a short pass.

This creates the following different chain reaction for the blue defending team:

1. **RCM** tracks the red midfielder's movement.

2. **RCB** covers and marks the red winger.

3. **CB**, **LCB** and **LWB** all shift across or back to retain balance in the defensive line.

THE ORGANISATION OF THE DEFENSIVE LINE

- The defensive line must always maintain a numerical superiority in the central zone.

- When defending with a back 4, the wing back on the opposite side must always be focussed on defending the opposing winger. However, the wing back closest to the ball area can deal with either the opposing winger or central midfielder.

- When defending with a back 5, we have shown how the wing back or the central midfielder have to react to press the opponents in their half. This leads to a chain reaction from the other players, depending on the movement of the opponents.

4. TACTICS AGAINST THE 4-3-1-2

4.1 - OVERCOMING THE FIRST LINE OF PRESSING (BUILD-UP PLAY FROM THE BACK)

Tactical Solutions to Build-up Play from the Back Against the 4-3-1-2 Formation

3 v 2 Advantage

LCB and RCB stay wide to increase the difficult for the red forwards to press

Created using SoccerTutor.com Tactics Manager

When building up play from the back against the 4-3-1-2, it is important to take advantage of the numerical superiority of 3 defenders against the 2 opposing forwards.

The 3 centre backs stay as open (wide) as possible to increase the difficulty for the 2 forwards to apply pressing and/or mark them.

As a general rule, it should be easy to find one of the wide centre backs in space as the free man. In this example, the right centre back

(**RCB**) receives from the middle centre back (**CB**) in a wide position and dribbles forward.

If the opposition decide to move their No.10 forward and apply a 3v3 press against the blue centre backs, they will then move slightly closer together and 1 or both wing backs drop back.

The aim will be to overcome the first line of pressing by passing to a wing back or the defensive midfielder - see pages 56 and 57 for tactical solutions in this situation.

4.2 - MOVING THE BALL IN BETWEEN THE OPPOSITION'S MIDFIELD AND DEFENSIVE LINES

A. Wide Centre Back's Options to Play Through the Opposition's Midfield

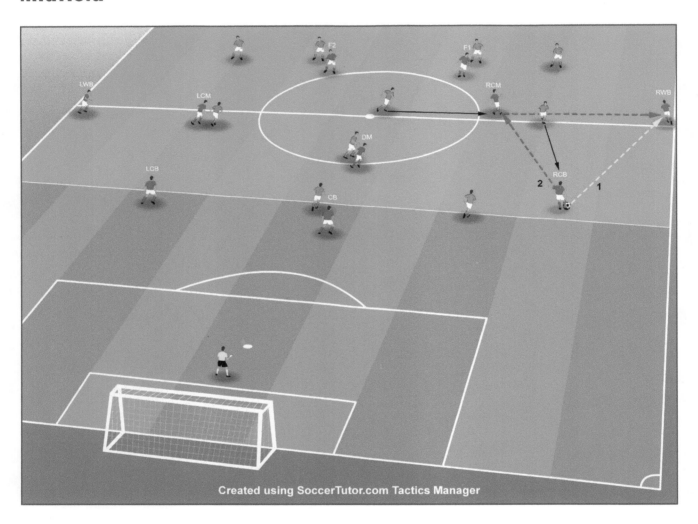

Created using SoccerTutor.com Tactics Manager

Following the right centre back (**RCB**) dribbling forward out of defence (see previous page), the aim is now to move the ball to a team-mate in between the opposition's midfield and defensive lines.

The right centre back (**RCB**) is being closed down by the opposing red team's left central midfielder. As the opposition's 4-3-1-2 formation lacks width in the midfield area, the aim is to play the ball to the right wing back (**RWB**).

These are the 2 Options for the RCB:

1. Pass directly to the right wing back (**RWB**).

2. Pass to the right wing back (**RWB**) via the right central midfielder (**RCM**).

NOTE: The choice of the options above mainly depends on how the opposing central midfielder presses and what passing lanes are available.

B. Switching Play to the Wing Back on the Weak Side when Pressed and the Opposition Are Compact in Midfield

If the opposition's central midfielder is able to quickly press the wing back (**RWB**) and his team-mates shift across, the space and options become limited for the ball carrier.

The new aim becomes to switch play to the wing back on the weak side. In this example, the **RWB** passes inside to the right central midfielder (**RCM**), who drops back to receive and switch the play with a long pass.

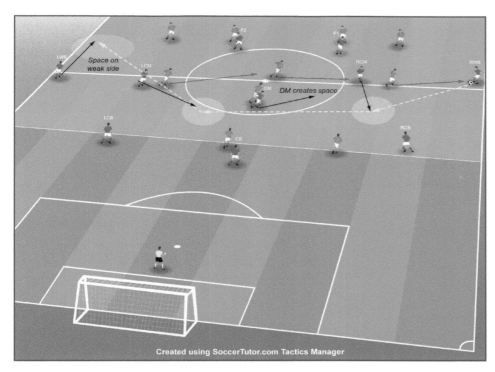

This is a variation of switching play without a long pass.

The defensive midfielder (**DM**) makes a forward movement, which creates space for the right central midfielder (**RCM**) to pass to the left central midfielder (**LCM**), who drops back to receive the sideways pass.

The **LCM** then passes out wide to the left wing back (**LWB**) to complete the switch.

C. Middle Centre Back's Options to Play Through the Opposition's Midfield when Pressed

Space created by DM

Created using SoccerTutor.com Tactics Manager

As the middle centre back (**CB**) dribbles forward out of defence, the defensive midfielder (**DM**) moves to the left to drag his marker away and create space in the centre of the pitch.

Therefore, the middle centre back (**CB**) starts to dribble the ball towards the right side of the pitch and is pressed by the opposing left central midfielder, who leaves his position.

The middle centre back's (**CB**) aim is now to move the ball to a team-mate in between the opposition's midfield and defensive lines.

The choice of which player to pass to may be determined by the way in which the red opponent presses him (body shape) and which passing lanes are open.

These are the 2 Options for the CB:

1. Pass to the right wing back (**RWB**) in space out wide.

2. Pass forward to the right central midfielder (**RCM**), who can receive and turn or pass to the right wing back (**RWB**), as shown in the diagram example.

D. Middle Centre Back's Options to Play Through the Opposition's Midfield when Not Pressed

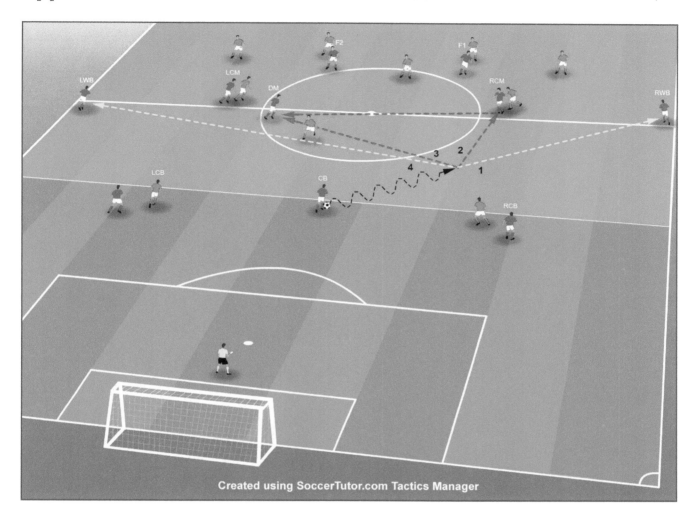

Created using SoccerTutor.com Tactics Manager

In this variation of the previous tactical situation, the opposing left central midfielder chooses not to press the ball carrier.

Therefore, the middle centre back (**CB**) has more options and tactical solutions to move the ball in between the opposition's midfield and defensive lines.

In this example, the middle centre back (**CB**) has again dribbled towards the right side of the pitch.

These are the 4 Options for the CB:

1. Pass to the right wing back (**RWB**), who is free in space in a wide position.

2. Pass forward to the right central midfielder (**RCM**), who can then pass across to the defensive midfielder (**DM**).

3. Direct diagonal pass to the defensive midfielder (**DM**).

4. Switch play with a long pass out wide to the left wing back (**LWB**).

4.3 - PLAYING IN BEHIND THE OPPOSITION'S DEFENSIVE LINE

Moving the Ball in Behind the Opposition's Defensive Line with the Wing Back in Possession

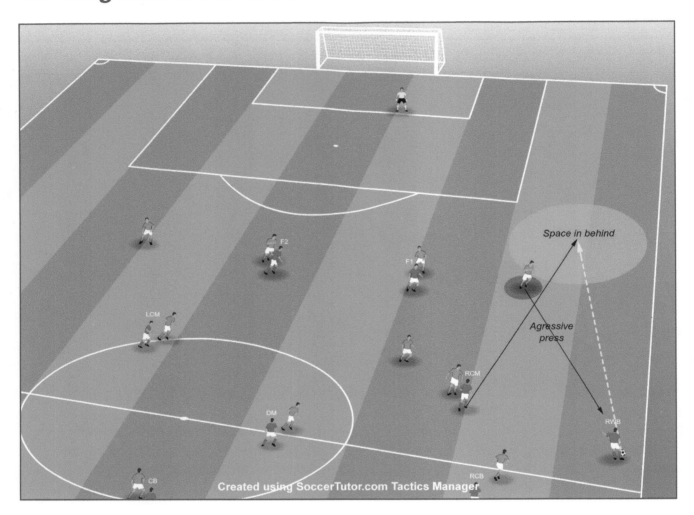

When the wing back is in possession, he must make decisions based on the pressing of the opponents:

1. If the right wing back (**RWB**) is pressed aggressively by the opposing left back, he passes into the space created for the right central midfielder (**RCM**) to receive in behind after a forward run.

2. If the opposing left back retains his position within the back 4, there is no space in behind

him to exploit. Therefore, the **RWB** simply passes inside for the **RCM** to receive.

KEY POINT: Unlike other formations, it is difficult for a central midfielder to receive in an advanced central position against the a 4-3-1-2, as the opposition have many players in the centre of the pitch. To play in behind the defensive line, the main objective is to use the wide areas, as shown in the diagram example above (RCM receives).

4.4 - PRESSING AGAINST THE 4-3-1-2 IN A 3-5-2 OR 3-5-1-1 SHAPE

When playing against the 4-3-1-2 formation (2 forwards and No.10), it is very important for the defensive midfielder (**DM**) to defend deeper than the central midfielders, making sure to mark the opposing No.10 tightly.

The first aim is to force play away from the opposing defensive midfielder. The central midfielders tighten their starting positions and block passing lanes towards the centre. The 2 forwards are positioned in line with each other.

A. Pressing the Centre Back Dribbling Forward with 3-5-2 Defensive Shape

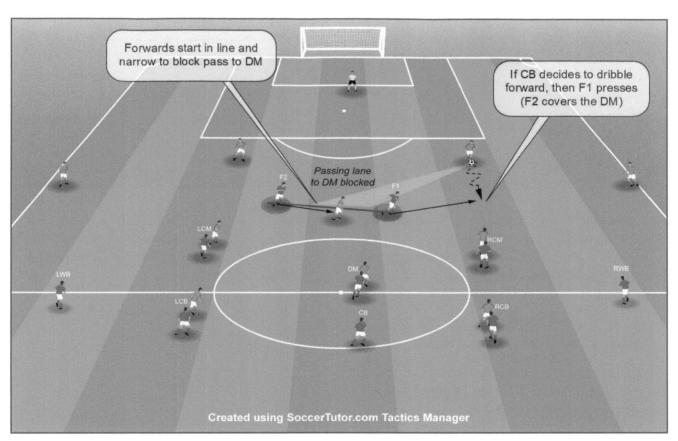

The 2 forwards are in line with each other and block the passing lane towards the red defensive midfielder.

This decision allows the red left centre back to dribble the ball forward.

When the red centre back moves forward, the closest blue forward (**F1**) moves to press the ball and the other forward (**F2**) shifts across at the same time to mark the opposing defensive midfielder.

B. Pressing the Centre Back Dribbling Forward with 3-5-1-1 Defensive Shape

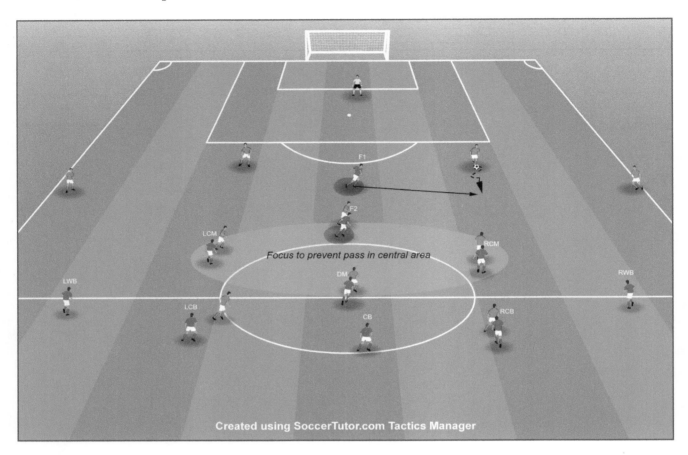

Created using SoccerTutor.com Tactics Manager

In this example, the blue team defend with a 3-5-1-1 shape and the 2 forwards are no longer in line with each other. Instead, **F2** is positioned behind **F1** and marks the opposing defensive midfielder.

The blue forwards again allow the red left centre back to dribble the ball forward.

When the red centre back moves forward, the closest blue forward (**F1**) moves to press the ball again and the other (**F2**) stays in the same position (marking the red defensive midfielder).

The main focus for the blue team is to prevent their opponents from passing to a team-mate in a central area. The 3 red central midfielders are all marked tightly.

C. The Central Midfielder Moves to Press the Opposing Full Back and the Wing Back Provides Cover

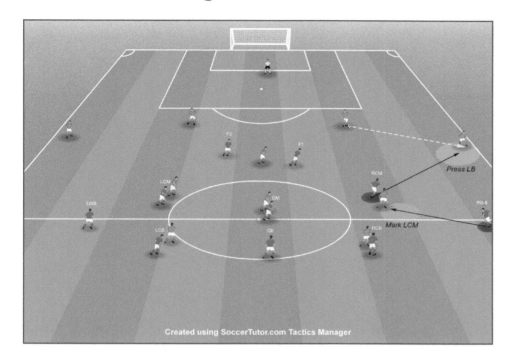

When the opposition build up play with the 4-3-1-2, the right central midfielder (**RCM**) and right wing back (**RWB**) must work together to mark the opposing full back and central midfielder on that side.

As the **RCM** moves forward to press the opposing left back, the **RWB** moves across and forward to tightly mark the opposing central midfielder.

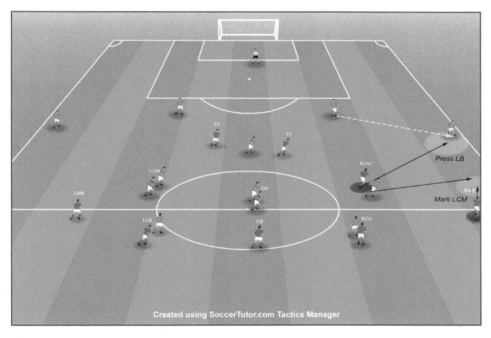

In this variation, the opposing red left central midfielder moves wide to try and receive from the red left back.

The right wing back (**RWB**) moves forward quickly to tightly mark the opposing central midfielder again.

NOTE: The example on this page is shown with the 2 forwards in a horizontal line within the 3-5-2 defensive shape, but the same conditions apply if changed to 1 forward behind the other in the 3-5-1-1 defensive shape.

D. The Wing Back Moves to Press the Opposing Full Back and the Central Midfielder Provides Cover

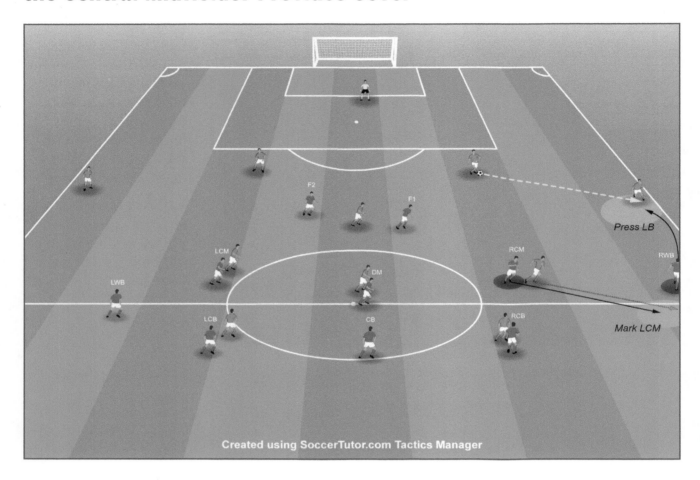

Created using SoccerTutor.com Tactics Manager

In this variation of the previous example, it is now the right wing back (**RWB**) who moves forward to press the opposing red left back.

The right wing back (**RWB**) should press with the correct body shape, to force the ball carrier to play inside, where the team have plenty of players and defensive stability.

It is now the right central midfielder's (**RCM**) responsibility to cover and mark the red opposing left central midfielder.

In this example, as the right wing back (**RWB**) moves forward to press the opposing left back, the opposing left central midfielder moves towards the side line.

The right central midfielder (**RCM**) tracks the movement and makes sure to closely mark the red midfielder, preventing him from receiving the ball.

4.5 - ORGANISATION OF THE DEFENSIVE LINE

Maintaining a Numerical Advantage at the Back and Defending the No.10 Against the 4-3-1-2

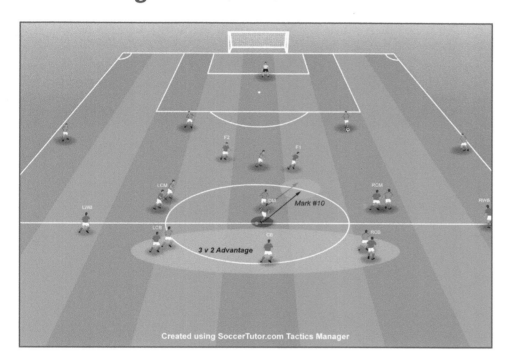

The defensive line must always maintain a numerical superiority in the central zone against the 2 forwards.

If the opposing No.10 moves to receive, this will be dealt with by the defensive midfielder (**DM**).

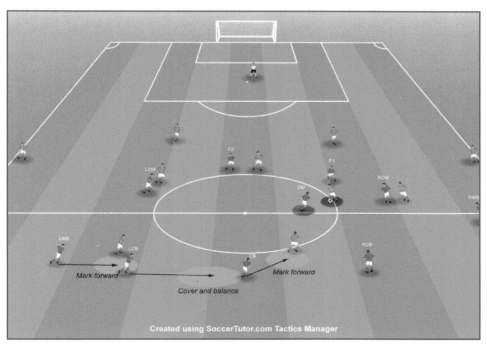

If the red No.10 is able to escape the defensive midfielder (**DM**) and receive a pass, the defensive line need to adjust their positions:

1. The **CB** marks the closest forward to the ball.

2. The **LCB** shifts across to provide cover and balance in the centre.

3. The **LWB** shifts across to mark the second forward.

5. TACTICS AGAINST THE 3-5-2

5.1 - OVERCOMING THE FIRST LINE OF PRESSING (BUILD-UP PLAY FROM THE BACK)

Tactical Solutions to Build-up Play from the Back Against the 3-5-2 Formation

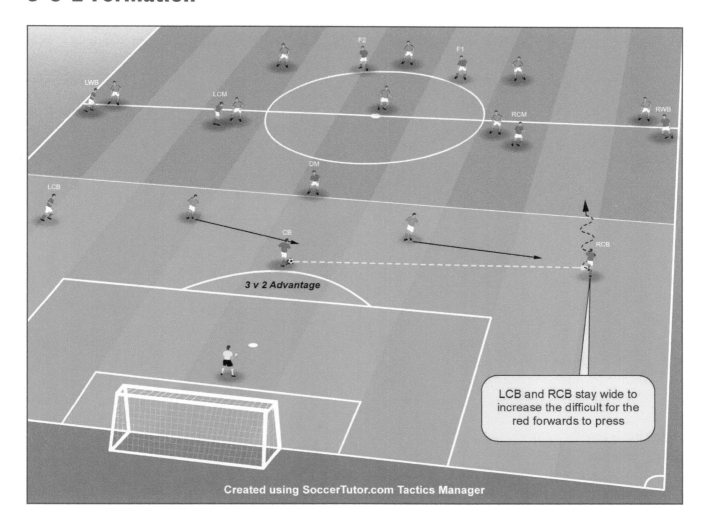

When building up play from the back against the 3-5-2, it is important to take advantage of the numerical superiority of 3 defenders against the 2 opposing forwards.

The 3 centre backs stay as open (wide) as possible to increase the difficulty for the 2 red forwards to apply pressing and/or mark them.

As a general rule, it should be easy to find one of the wide centre backs in space as the free man. In this example, the right centre back (**RCB**) receives from the middle centre back (**CB**) in a wide position and dribbles forward.

5.2 - MOVING THE BALL IN BETWEEN THE OPPOSITION'S MIDFIELD AND DEFENSIVE LINES

A. Wide Centre Back's Options to Play Through the Opposition's Midfield

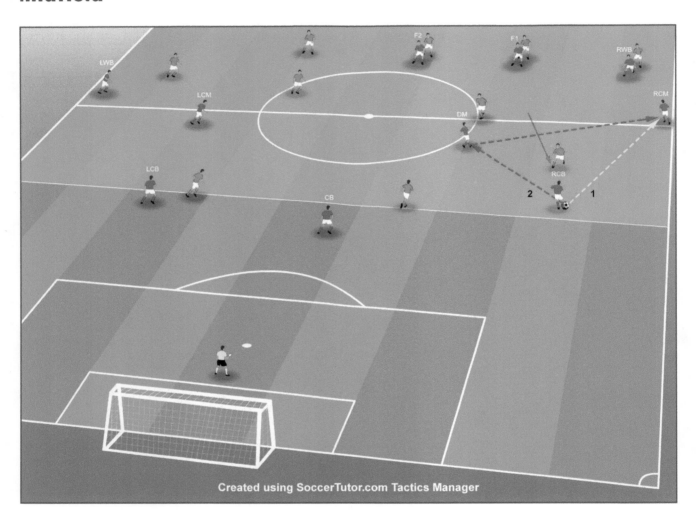

Created using SoccerTutor.com Tactics Manager

Following the right centre back (**RCB**) dribbling forward out of defence (see previous page), his aim is now to move the ball to a team-mate in between the opposition's midfield and defensive lines.

When building up play against the 3-5-2, the wing backs (**LWB** and **RWB**) move up against the opposing wing backs in advanced positions, up against the defensive line. The central midfielder (**RCM**) on the ball side moves into a wide position as a potential receiver.

The aim is to move the ball in between the opposition's midfield and defensive lines and then play a through pass in behind.

These are the 2 Options for the RCB:

1. Pass to the right central midfielder (**RCM**) in a wide position.

2. Pass to the right central midfielder (**RCM**) via the defensive midfielder (**DM**), who is positioned close to the ball area.

B. Switching Play to the Wing Back on the Weak Side when Pressed and the Opposition Are Compact in Midfield

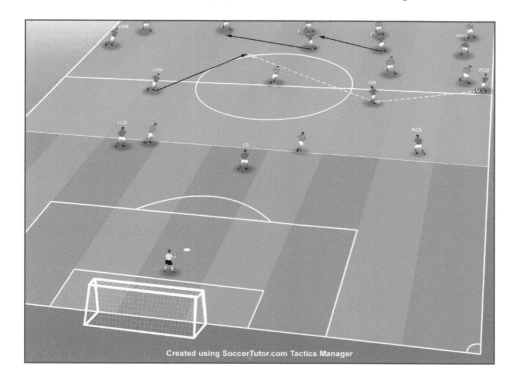

In this example, the opposition's central midfielder is able to quickly press the blue central midfielder (**RCM**), so the space and options become limited.

The new aim becomes to switch play to the wing back on the weak side. The **RCM** passes inside to the defensive midfielder (**DM**), who plays a diagonal pass for the forward run of the left central midfielder (**LCM**) in between the lines.

C. Wide Centre Back's Options when the Opposing Wing Back Moves Forward and in Behind

If the opposing left wing back moves forward to mark the right central midfielder (**RCM**), the right centre back (**RCB**) has 2 options:

1. Pass in behind to the advanced wing back (**RWB**) if the opposing defenders have any delay in shifting across.

2. Pass to the forward (**F1**) to exploit the 2 v 2 situation the forwards have in the centre.

D. Middle Centre Back's Options to Play Through the Opposition's Midfield when Pressed

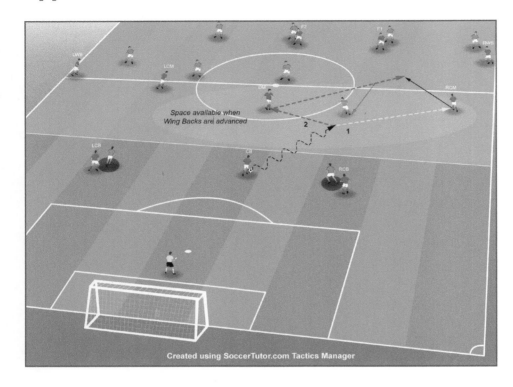

With the wing backs in advanced positions, there is more space available in midfield.

As the middle centre back (**CB**) dribbles forward out of defence, the opposing central midfielder moves forward to press him.

2 Options for CB:

1. Pass to the central midfielder (**RCM**).

2. Pass to the **RCM** via the defensive midfielder (**DM**).

E. Defensive Midfielder's Options to Play Through the Opposition's Midfield when Not Pressed

In this variation, the defensive midfielder (**DM**) dribbles the ball forward and the opposing red left central midfielder chooses not to press the ball carrier.

The defensive midfielder (**DM**) plays a diagonal pass for the diagonal run of the right central midfielder (**RCM**), who receives between the line.

See the following page for **RCM's** options...

5.3 - PLAYING IN BEHIND THE OPPOSITION'S DEFENSIVE LINE

Central Midfielder's Options to Play in Behind the Defensive Line After Receiving Between the Lines

Created using SoccerTutor.com Tactics Manager

Following the right central midfielder (**RCM**) receiving between the lines (see previous page), his aim is now to move the ball to a team-mate in behind the opposition's defensive line.

As the **RCM** dribbles forward, the 2 blue forwards make movements to create doubt for the opposing wide centre backs, while the wing back (**LWB**) makes a cutting run in between the red wing back and right centre back.

These are the 4 Options for the RCM:

1. If the opposing right centre back tightens their position in the centre, there is space to pass for the cutting run of the **LWB**.

2. If the opposing wing back shifts inside, there will be a pass out wide to the **LWB** available.

3. If the opposing wide centre backs move wider to cover the movement of the forwards (**F1** and **F2**), the **RCM** can continue to dribble forward and commit the defenders (3v3).

4. If the opposing left centre back stays central and the left wing back doesn't move inside, space is free for the **RWB** to make a run in behind and receive.

5.4 - PRESSING AND DEFENSIVE ORGANISATION

Against the 3-5-2 formation, the 3 midfielders must all be positioned in a line together and the focus is on preventing the opposing defensive midfielder from receiving the ball in the centre of the pitch.

The 2 forwards block the passing lane towards the red defensive midfielder.

The coach should be focussed on the combined movement of the central midfielder (**RCM**), the

wing back (**RWB**), the defensive midfielder (**DM**) and the wide centre back (**RCB**).

The central midfielder (**RCM**) moves forward to press the opposing centre back and tries to direct him inside, where there are plenty of players and defensive stability. The defensive reactions of the wing back (**RWB**) and defensive midfielder (**DM**) depend on the movement of the opposing central midfielder and winger.

A. The Central Midfielder Moves to Press the Opposing Wide Centre Back and the Defensive Midfielder Provides Cover

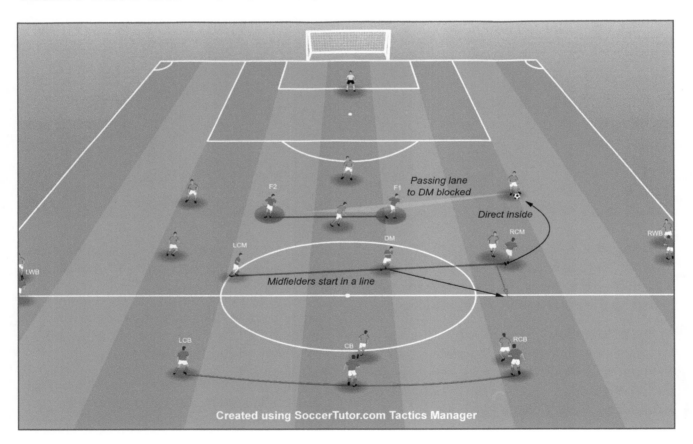

If the opposing red left wing back stays in his position and the left central midfielder moves forward (as shown), the blue right wing back

(**RWB**) stays in position to mark his direct opponent and the defensive midfielder (**DM**) tracks the run of the central midfielder.

B. The Central Midfielder Moves to Press the Opposing Wide Centre Back and the Other Players Shift to Provide Cover

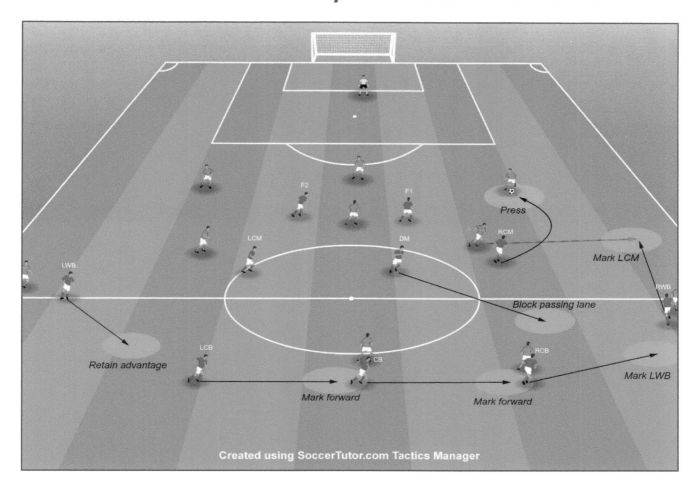

Created using SoccerTutor.com Tactics Manager

In this example, the opposing red left central midfielder moves across into a wide position, to try and receive the next pass.

This creates the following different chain reaction for the blue defending team:

1. The right wing back (**RWB**) tracks the red left central midfielder's movement and moves forward to mark him.

2. The defensive midfielder (**DM**) drops back in front of the defence to block any passing lanes towards the forwards.

3. The right centre back (**RCB**) shifts across to mark the opposing left wing back.

4. The middle centre back (**CB**) and the left centre back (**LCB**) shift across to tighten the defensive line and mark the 2 red forwards.

5. The left wing back (**LWB**) drops back to retain a numerical superiority at the back.

6. TACTICS AGAINST THE 3-4-3

6.1 - OVERCOMING THE FIRST LINE OF PRESSING (BUILD-UP PLAY FROM THE BACK)

A. The Ball is Moved Easily Between the 3 Centre Backs Against the 1 Opposing Forward

3 v 1 Advantage

LCB and RCB are distant enough to make it difficult for the forward to press

Created using SoccerTutor.com Tactics Manager

When building up play from the back against the 3-4-3, the team has a 3v1 numerical superiority against the 1 forward.

The 3 centre backs are distant from each other (but not too much) so it's difficult for the red forward to apply pressing and/or mark them.

Usually in this situation, a wide centre back is able to receive in space and exploit the situation to move the team forward and overcome the first line of pressing.

In this example, the middle centre back (**CB**) is put under pressure by the red forward and passes to the right centre back (**RCB**).

These are the <u>2 Options</u> for the RCB:

1. If the red forward is unable to press the **RCB**, he can dribble the ball forward freely.

2. If the red forward is able to apply pressure, the **RCB** can easily pass to the defensive midfielder (**DM**), who is free in the centre.

B. Tactical Solution to Build-up When the Opposition Wingers Move Up to Press the Centre Backs

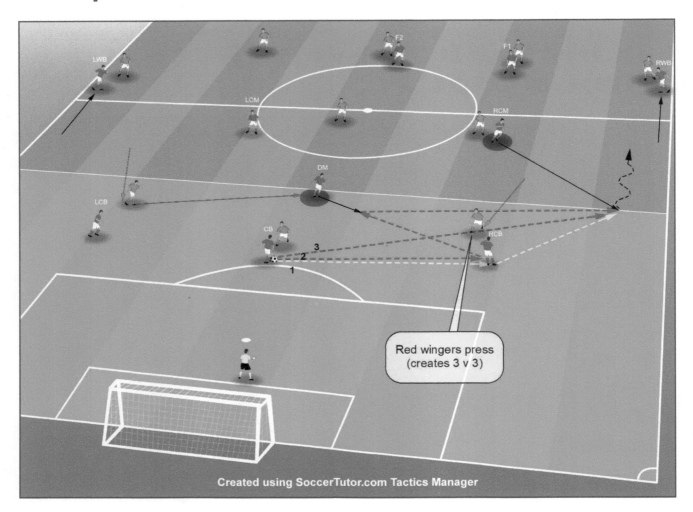

Red wingers press
(creates 3 v 3)

Created using SoccerTutor.com Tactics Manager

If the opposing team decide to move their wingers into advanced positions to create 3v3, the blue team must quickly recreate a numerical superiority at the back to build-up play:

1. The 3 defenders tighten up slightly.

2. The wing backs (**LWB** and **RWB**) push forward into advanced positions, right up against their direct markers.

3. The central midfielder on the ball side (**RCM** in diagram) drops back into a wide position to receive.

The aim for the blue defenders is to play the ball to the central midfielder (**RCM**) or the defensive midfielder (**DM**), as there is plenty of space behind the opposition's attacking line.

These are the **3 Options** for the blue team to successfully overcome the first line of pressing from the 3 red attackers:

1. The **RCM** drops back. The **CB** passes to the **RCB**, who then passes out wide to the **RCM**.

2. The **DM** drops back. **CB** passes to **RCB**, who passes to the **DM**. The **DM** then passes out wide to the **RCM**.

3. If the opposing winger is closely marking the **RCB** and there is a clear passing lane, the **CB** passes directly to the **RCM**.

NOTE: The choice of the options above mainly depends on how the opposing players press and what passing lanes are available.

C. Tactical Solution When the Opposition Wingers Move Up to Press: Defensive Midfielder Drops Back into Defensive Line

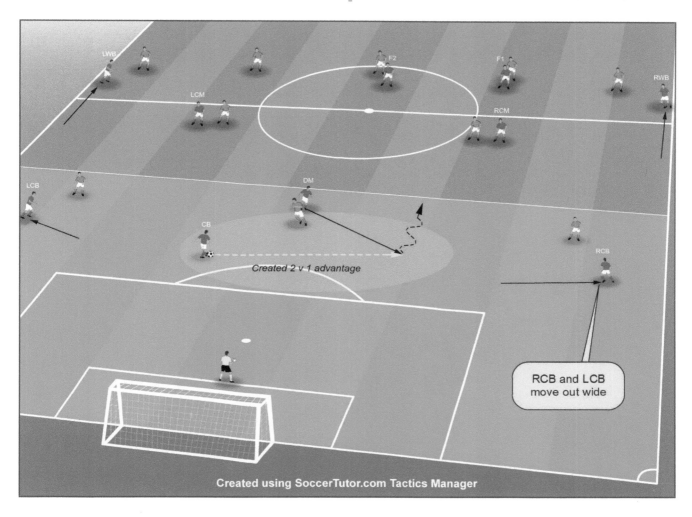

Created using SoccerTutor.com Tactics Manager

In this variation, the wide centre backs (**LCB** and **RCB**) push very wide to drag their markers (red wingers) away and create more space in the centre of the pitch.

The 2 wing backs (**LWB** and **RWB**) are pushed forward into advanced positions, occupying their direct opponents.

The 2 central midfielders (**LCM** and **RCM**) are in their starting positions, also occupying their direct opponents.

In this example, the defensive midfielder (**DM**) is able to drop back into the defensive line to create a 2v1 numerical advantage in the centre and receive from the middle centre back (**CB**).

From there, the defensive midfielder (**DM**) is able to dribble forward into space, looking to then move the ball in between the opposition's midfield and defensive lines.

6.2 - MOVING THE BALL IN BETWEEN THE OPPOSITION'S MIDFIELD AND DEFENSIVE LINES

A. Wide Centre Back's Options to Play Through the Opposition's Midfield

Created using SoccerTutor.com Tactics Manager

In this first example, the right centre back (**RCB**) has possession. The wing back (**RWB**) pushes right up to force his direct opponent to be in the defensive line and the right central midfielder (**RCM**) is in a wide position.

The right centre back (**RCB**) is being closed down by the opposing red team's left winger and the blue team aim to move the ball to the right central midfielder (**RCM**) in between the lines, as he is free of marking.

These are the 2 Options for the RCB:

1. Pass directly to the right central midfielder (**RCM**).

2. Pass to the right central midfielder (**RCM**) via the defensive midfielder (**DM**).

NOTE: The choice of the options above mainly depends on how the opposing winger presses and what passing lanes are available.

B. Wide Centre Back Uses the Defensive Midfielder as a Link Player to Move the Ball in Between the Lines

Created using SoccerTutor.com Tactics Manager

If the opposition's central midfielder is able to quickly press the centre back (**RCB**), he passes to the defensive midfielder (**DM**) who has **2 Options** to move the ball to a team-mate in between the lines:

1. Pass through the gap left by the red central midfielder to the **RCM**, who moves inside to receive.

2. Diagonal pass for the forward run of the **LCM**.

C. Central Midfielder's Options to Move the Ball to the Opposite Central Midfielder in Between the Lines

Created using SoccerTutor.com Tactics Manager

In this variation, the right central midfielder (**RCM**) is in possession after dropping back to receive and the opposition's wingers are behind the ball.

The **RCM** is pressed by the red central midfielder and there is lots of space in the middle of the pitch.

The **RCM** passes inside to the defensive midfielder (**DM**), who passes to the **LCM** in between the lines and free in space.

D. Wide Centre Back's Options when the Opposing Wing Back Moves Forward and Out in Behind

If the opposing left wing back moves forward to mark the right central midfielder (**RCM**), the right centre back (**RCB**) has **2 Options**:

1. Pass in behind to the advanced wing back (**RWB**), if the opposing defenders have any delay in shifting across.

2. Pass to the forward (**F1**) to exploit the 2v2 situation the forwards have in the centre.

E. Defensive Midfielder's Options to Play Through the Opposition's Midfield when Pressed

With the wing backs in advanced positions, there is more space available in midfield.

As the defensive midfielder (**DM**) dribbles forward, the opposing central midfielder moves forward to press him.

2 Options for DM:

1. Pass to the central midfielder (**RCM**).

2. Pass to the **RCM** via the left central midfielder (**LCM**).

6.3 - PLAYING IN BEHIND THE OPPOSITION'S DEFENSIVE LINE

Central Midfielder's Options to Play in Behind the Defensive Line After Receiving Between the Lines

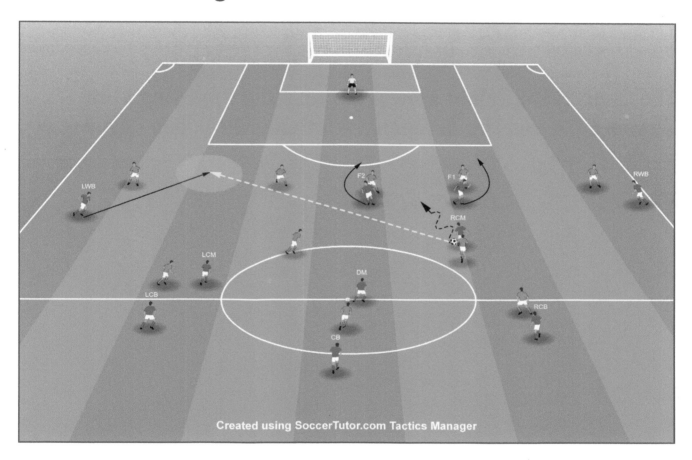

Created using SoccerTutor.com Tactics Manager

The right central midfielder (**RCM**) receives between the lines (see previous page), with the aim to move the ball to a team-mate in behind the opposition's defensive line.

As the **RCM** dribbles forward, the 2 blue forwards make movements to create doubt for the opposing wide centre backs, while the left wing back (**LWB**) makes a cutting run in between the red centre back and wing back.

These are the 4 Options for the RCM:

1. If the opposing wide centre back tightens their position in the centre, there is space to pass for the cutting run of the **LWB**.

2. If the opposing wing back shifts inside, there will be a pass out wide to the **LWB** available.

3. If the opposing wide centre backs move wider to cover the movement of the forwards (**F1** and **F2**), the **RCM** can continue to dribble forward and commit the defenders in a 3 v 3 situation.

4. If the opposing left centre back stays central and the left wing back doesn't move inside, space is free for the **RWB** to make a run in behind and receive.

6.4 - PRESSING AND DEFENSIVE ORGANISATION

Against the 3-4-3 formation, the 3 midfielders must all be positioned in a line together and the coach must define the behaviour of the 2 forwards against the 3 opposing 3 centre backs:

1. The 2 forwards (**F1** and **F2**) shift their starting positions slightly to one side of the pitch.

2. The 2 forwards mark 2 of the centre backs tightly and try to isolate the third.

3. Freedom and time is granted for one of the opposing wide centre backs, so a midfielder will have to move forward and press them.

The Central Midfielder Moves to Press the Opposing Wide Centre Back and the Defensive Midfielder Provides Cover

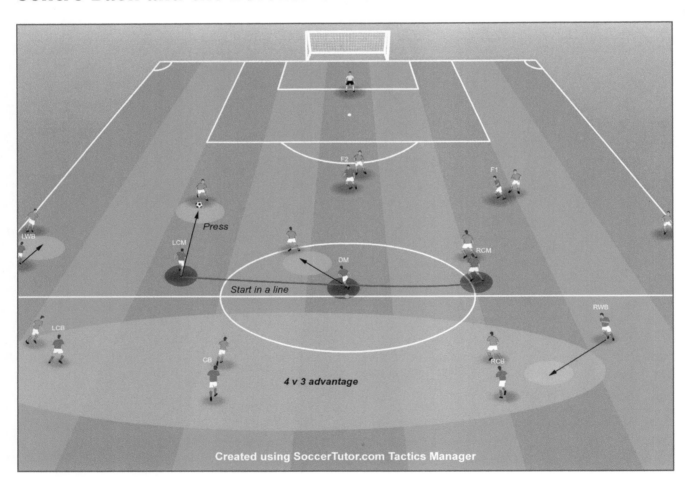

The central midfielder on that side (**LCM**) presses the red right centre back (ball carrier). The defensive midfielder (**DM**) moves forward to close down one of the opposing central midfielders and the other central midfielder is marked by the **RCM**, as shown.

As the play is coming down the blue team's left, the left wing back (**LWB**) marks his direct opponent and the right wing back (**RWB**) on the weak side drops back to create a back 4 and a 4v3 numerical superiority in defence.

6.5 - ORGANISATION OF THE DEFENSIVE LINE

Defensive Movements to Provide Cover and Balance Against the 3-4-3 Formation

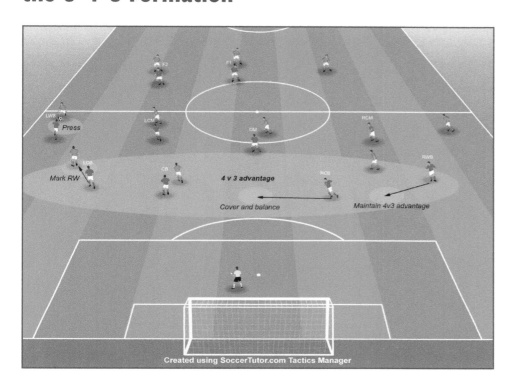

The defensive line must always maintain a numerical superiority against the opposing attackers.

Against the 3-4-3, they must retain a 4 v 3 advantage at all times.

In this example, the **LWB** is contesting the ball, so the **LCB** marks the red right winger, the **CB** marks the forward, the **RCB** shifts into the centre and the **RWB** drops back to create a back 4.

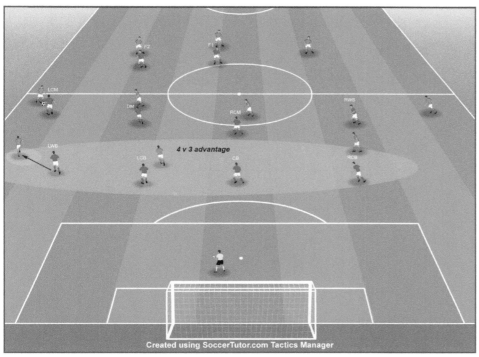

In this variation of the same tactical situation, the **LCM** is contesting the opposing right wing back (ball carrier).

Therefore, the blue **LWB** marks the red right winger and the **RWB** can stay in his midfield position.

The **LCB** marks the red forward, the **CB** stays in his central position and the **RCB** covers the red left winger.

CHAPTER 3

TRAINING SESSION EXAMPLES

KEY POINTS FOR COACHES TO CONSIDER

1. The practices displayed in this chapter should only serve as a starting point for coaches.

2. The practices must then be adapted depending on many factors, including the age/level of the players, the characteristics of the players, the time available, the training structures and the team/club objectives.

3. Adapt and modify the teaching process.

TRAINING SESSION 1:

BUILD-UP PLAY FROM THE BACK

I. Unopposed Build-up Play Passing Warm-up

Variation I - Wide Centre Back Dribbles Forward

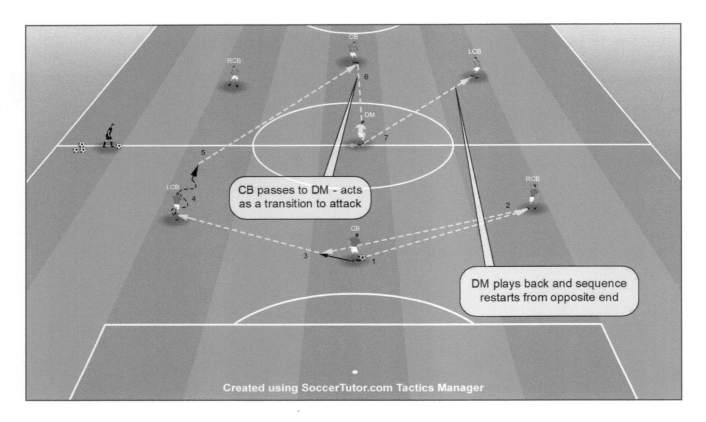

CB passes to DM - acts as a transition to attack

DM plays back and sequence restarts from opposite end

Created using SoccerTutor.com Tactics Manager

NOTE: This practice shows just the 3 centre backs building up play with the defensive midfielder, but you can also add the wing backs.

Practice Description (Variation 1)

- Using the middle area of the pitch, there are 2 sets of 3 centre backs either side of the defensive midfielder (**DM**) in the centre.

- We have displayed 3 different variations of how to build-up from the back (see next 2 pages) for this practice, but there are many more you can use.

- The practice starts with the 3 blue centre backs circulating the ball using a maximum of 2 touches.

- One of the centre backs (**LCB** in diagram example) receives and dribbles forward with the ball.

- The left centre back (**LCB**) then passes to one of the red centre backs on the other side.

- The red centre back that receives (**CB** in diagram example) plays a first time pass to the defensive midfielder (**DM**), which acts as a quick transition to attack.

- The defensive midfielder (**DM**) passes the ball back to a different red player and the practice sequence restarts from the opposite end.

Variation 2 - Centre Back Runs Forward to Receive Lay-off from Defensive Midfielder

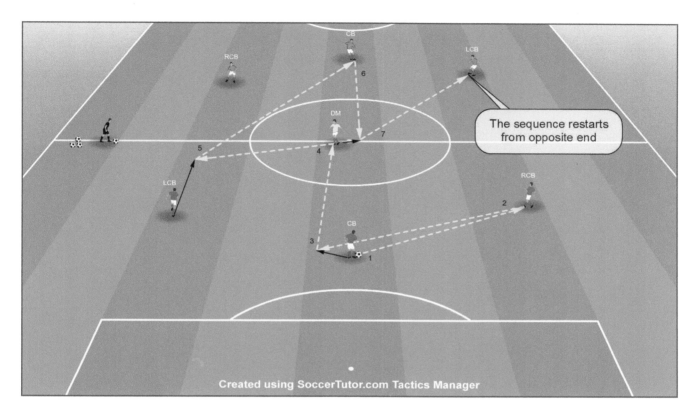

The sequence restarts from opposite end

Created using SoccerTutor.com Tactics Manager

Practice Description (Variation 2)

- The practice starts with the 3 blue centre backs circulating the ball using a maximum of 2 touches.

- One of the centre backs (**CB** in diagram example) **receives and passes forward to the defensive midfielder (DM).**

- The defensive midfielder (**DM**) lays the ball off for the forward run of a different centre back (**LCB** in diagram example).

- The left centre back (**LCB**) then passes to one of the red centre backs on the other side.

- The red centre back that receives (**CB** in diagram example) **plays a first time pass to the defensive midfielder (DM), which acts as a quick transition to attack.**

- The defensive midfielder (**DM**) passes the ball back to a different red player and the practice sequence restarts from the opposite end.

Variation 3 - Diagonal Aerial Pass (Switch of Play)

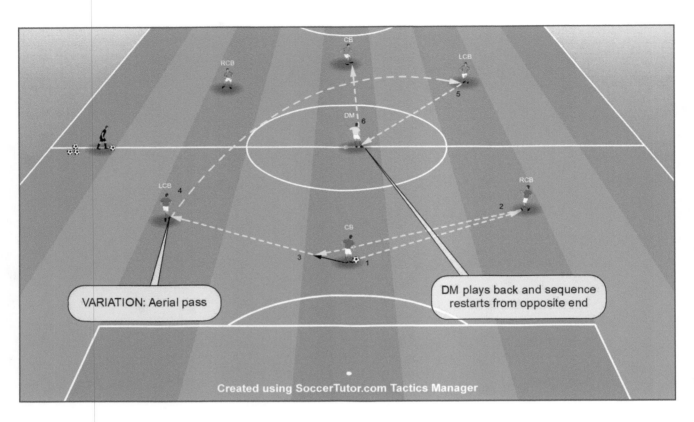

VARIATION: Aerial pass

DM plays back and sequence restarts from opposite end

Created using SoccerTutor.com Tactics Manager

Practice Description (Variation 3)

- The practice starts with the 3 blue centre backs circulating the ball using a maximum of 2 touches.

- One of the centre backs (**LCB** in diagram example) receives and switches play to the other side with a diagonal aerial pass to the red left centre back (**LCB**).

- The red centre back that receives (**LCB** in diagram example) plays a first time pass to the defensive midfielder (**DM**), which acts as a quick transition to attack.

- The defensive midfielder (**DM**) passes the ball back to a different red player and the practice sequence restarts from the opposite end.

2. Build-up Play from the Back in a Dynamic 8 (+GK) v 6 Game

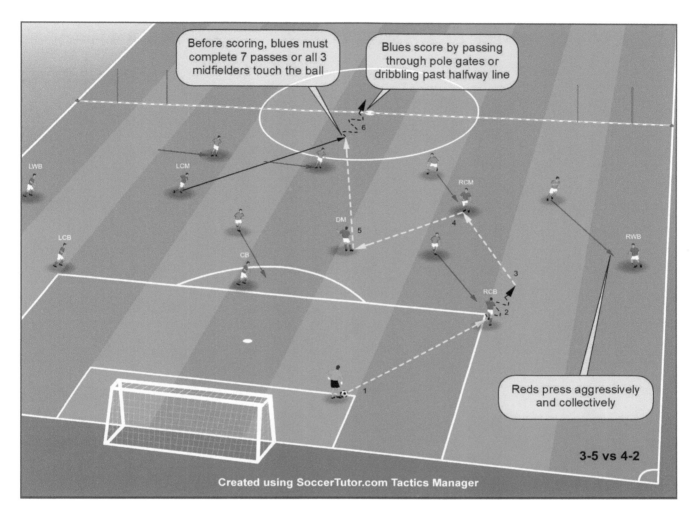

Before scoring, blues must complete 7 passes or all 3 midfielders touch the ball

Blues score by passing through pole gates or dribbling past halfway line

Reds press aggressively and collectively

3-5 vs 4-2

Created using SoccerTutor.com Tactics Manager

Practice Description

- Using half a pitch, the blue team have 8 outfield players (3-5 formation) and a GK.

- The red defending team have 6 players in a 4-2 formation from the 4-4-2, but this can be changed to suit any formation.

- The practice starts with a short pass from the GK to one of the 3 centre backs.

- The blue team try to exploit their numerical advantage to build-up play and overcome the pressing of the red defending team.

- The red team press aggressively and collectively to try to win the ball.

- The blue team score either by dribbling past the halfway line (as in diagram example) or by passing the ball through one of the 2 pole gates.

- Before a goal can be scored, the blue team must either complete 7 passes or all 3 central midfielders must have touched the ball (**DM**, **LCM** and **RCM**).

- If the reds win the ball, they launch a counter attack and try to score past the blue team's GK as quickly as possible.

3. Build-up Play Through the Lines in a 3 Zone Conditioned Practice

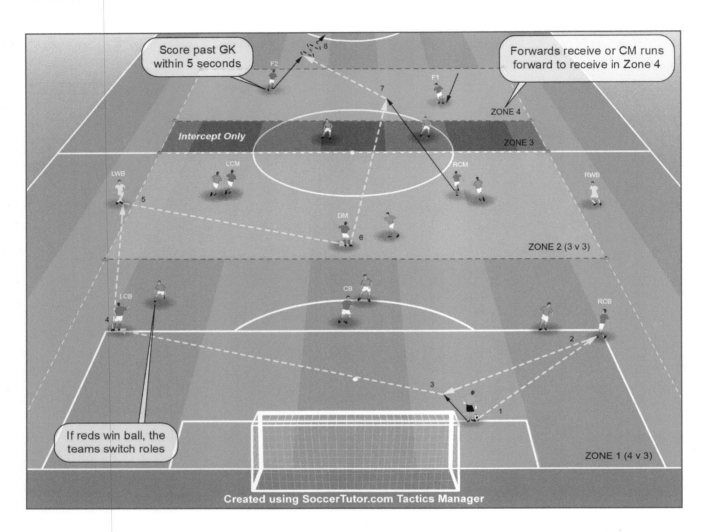

Practice Description

- Mark out 4 horizontal zones as shown. Outside these zones, there are wide channels where only the neutral wing backs play.

- The practice starts with the GK in Zone 1. The 3 blue centre backs utilise the yellow neutral wing backs to move the ball to one of the 3 midfielders in Zone 2.

- **NOTE:** If a blue centre back is able to receive free of pressure from the 3 red opponents, he can dribble forward into Zone 2 to create a numerical advantage (4v3) in there.

- In Zone 2, the 3 blue midfielders utilise their advantage with the 2 neutral wing backs (and possibly 1 defender).

- The aim in Zone 2 is to pass to a player in Zone 4, which can either be for a central midfielder's forward run (**RCM** in diagram example) or a forward who drops back.

- Before this can happen, a neutral wing back (**LWB** in diagram example) must have touched the ball during the build-up.

- The 2 red players in Zone 3 can only intercept passes and must stay within their zone.

- The forward that receives beyond Zone 4 must score past the GK within 5 seconds.

- If the red defending team win the ball at any time, the teams switch roles and the practice starts again from the GK.

4. Build-up from the Back and Pass in Behind the Midfield Line in a Tactical 4 Zone Practice

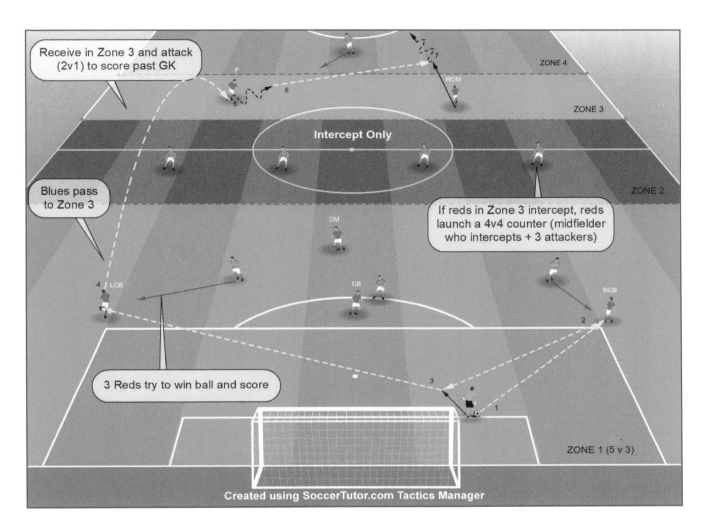

Receive in Zone 3 and attack (2v1) to score past GK

Blues pass to Zone 3

Intercept Only

If reds in Zone 3 intercept, reds launch a 4v4 counter (midfielder who intercepts + 3 attackers)

3 Reds try to win ball and score

ZONE 4

ZONE 3

ZONE 2

ZONE 1 (5 v 3)

Created using SoccerTutor.com Tactics Manager

Practice Description

- This is a positional practice to build-up play and search for a way to play in behind the opposition's midfield line. Using a full pitch, 4 zones are marked out as shown.

- The practice starts with the GK's short pass in Zone 1 and the blue team use their 5v3 numerical advantage (including GK) as they build-up play from the back.

- The aim is to overcome the pressing of the 3 red attackers and pass to a team-mate in Zone 3 (**LCB** to **F** in diagram example). If the reds win the ball in Zone 1, they try to score past the GK as quickly as possible.

- If **F** or **RCM** receive successfully within Zone 3, they then attack in a 2v1 situation against the 1 red defender and try to score in the goal past the GK in Zone 4.

- The 4 red midfielders in Zone 3 can only intercept passes and if they succeed, they launch a 4v4 counter attack (1 midfielder who makes the interception + 3 attackers) and try to score as quickly as possible.

- **KEY POINT:** This practice is useful for training build-up play from the back against opposing teams that use ultra-offensive (aggressive) pressing.

TRAINING SESSION 2:
PLAYING THROUGH THE LINES

1. Playing in Behind the Line in a 3 v 3 Small Sided Game with 6 Mini Goals

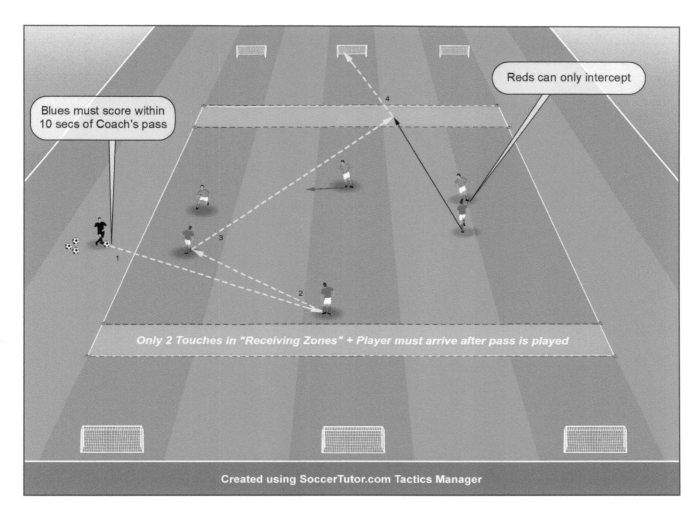

Practice Description

- Mark out a 20 x 30 yard area with 3 yard "Receiving Zones" at each end. Outside, there are 6 mini goals as shown.

- The practice starts with the Coach's pass to either team and we play a 3v3 game.

- The team in possession (blue) have unlimited touches and the defending team (red) can only win the ball by intercepting it and are not allowed to tackle their opponents.

- The aim for the blue team is to successfully pass to a team-mate within the "Receiving Zone" and score.

To score a goal, the teams have to meet all of these **3 Conditions**:

1. Teams must score within 10 seconds of receiving the Coach's pass.

2. Only 2 touches allowed in the "Receiving Zone" (receive and shoot).

3. The receiver in the "Receiving Zone" must arrive there with a forward run/movement and must not already be positioned in there before the final pass is played.

Variation - 3 v 3 (+2) Small Sided Game

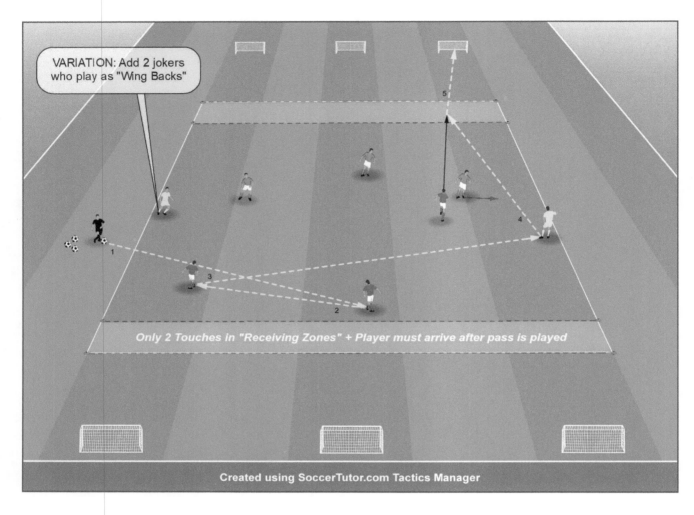

VARIATION: Add 2 jokers who play as "Wing Backs"

Only 2 Touches in "Receiving Zones" + Player must arrive after pass is played

Created using SoccerTutor.com Tactics Manager

Practice Description

- This is a variation of the previous practice with 2 jokers added. They play in wide positions to represent wing backs.

- The practice starts with the Coach's pass to either team and we play a 3v3 (+2) game.

- The rules and conditions are exactly the same as the previous variation (see previous page) but now the team in possession can utilise their numerical advantage with help from the 2 jokers.

- The jokers are not allowed to receive within the "Receiving Zones" and score.

- If the red team intercept the ball, they try to score in the same way, with help from the jokers.

- When a goal is scored or the ball goes out of play, the Coach passes a new ball to the other team.

2. Playing Through the Lines in an 8v8 Game with 6 Mini Goals

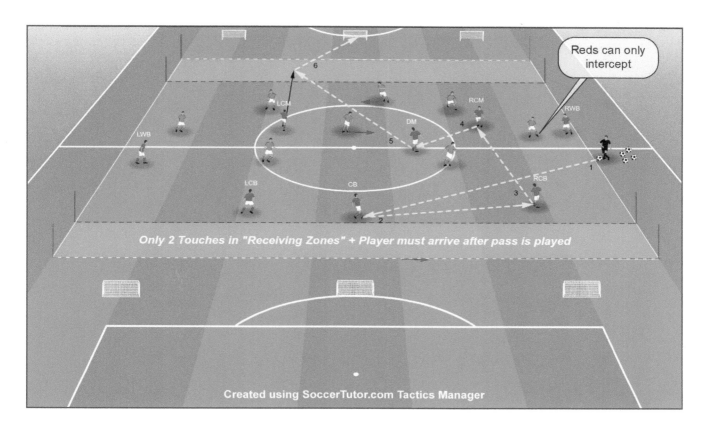

Practice Description

- Using a full pitch, mark out a main area + 2 "Receiving Zones" (yellow highlighted areas) and position 6 mini goals, as shown.

- The practice starts with the Coach's pass to a centre back and we play an 8v8 game.

- The team in possession (blue) have unlimited touches and the defending team (red) can only win the ball by intercepting it and are not allowed to tackle their opponents.

- The aim for the blues is to build-up, play through the red's pressure and play in behind for a central midfielder (**LCM** or **RCM**) to time a run, receive in the "Receiving Zone" and score.

To score a goal, the teams have to meet both of these **2 Conditions**:

1. Only 2 touches allowed in the "Receiving Zone" (receive and shoot).

2. The receiver (**LCM** in diagram example) **must arrive in the "Receiving Zone" with a forward run/movement and must not already be positioned in there before the final pass is played.**

3. Build-up and Playing Through the Midfield Line Patterns of Play

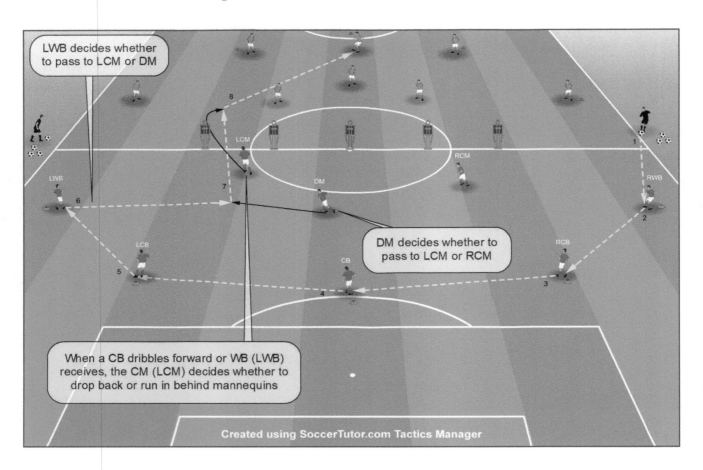

Practice Description

- On a full pitch, there are 2 teams in a 3-5 formation (from the 3-5-2) on opposite sides.

- The practice starts with the Coach's pass to any of the 3 centre backs or 2 wing backs and that team circulate the ball around at the back, as shown.

- When a centre back dribbles the ball forward out from the back or the ball reaches a wing back (**LWB** in diagram example), the central midfielder on that side decides whether to drop back (unmark) and receive a short pass or move forward into a position behind the opposition's midfield line (mannequins).

- In this example, the left central midfielder (**LCM**) makes a forward run in behind the midfield line to receive.

- The wing back (**LWB**) then decides whether to play a forward pass immediately to the **LCM** or pass the to the defensive midfielder (**DM**), who moves across to receive.

- If the defensive midfielder (**DM**) receives, he then decides whether to play a forward pass immediately (as shown in diagram) or pass to the other central midfielder (**RCM**). If the **RCM** receives, he must play a forward pass in between the midfield line (mannequins).

- To complete the sequence, the Coach makes sure the central midfielder (**LCM**) receives with an open body shape (facing forward) and passes to a red centre back.

- The reds then have the same objective in the opposite direction.

Variation - Central Midfielder Drops Back

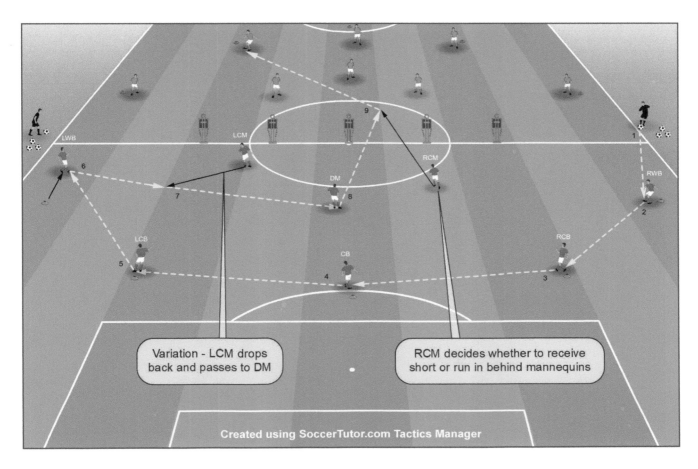

Variation - LCM drops back and passes to DM

RCM decides whether to receive short or run in behind mannequins

Created using SoccerTutor.com Tactics Manager

Practice Description

- In this variation (see previous page), **the central midfielder (LCM) drops back to receive a short pass from the wing back (LWB) instead of making a forward run.**

- The defensive midfielder (**DM**) does not shift across and stays in his central position.

- The left central midfielder (**LCM**) receives the short pass and then passes to the defensive midfielder (**DM**).

- In this situation, the right central midfielder (**RCM**) must decide whether to make an unmarking movement and receive a short pass or make a forward run.

- As shown in the diagram example, the right central midfielder (**RCM**) makes a run in behind the opposition's midfield line (mannequins) and receives the defensive midfielder's (**DM**) immediate forward pass.

- To complete the sequence, the Coach makes sure the central midfielder (**RCM**) receives with an open body shape (facing forward) and passes to a red centre back.

- The reds then have the same objective in the opposite direction.

4. Playing Through the Centre and Finish in a Functional Practice

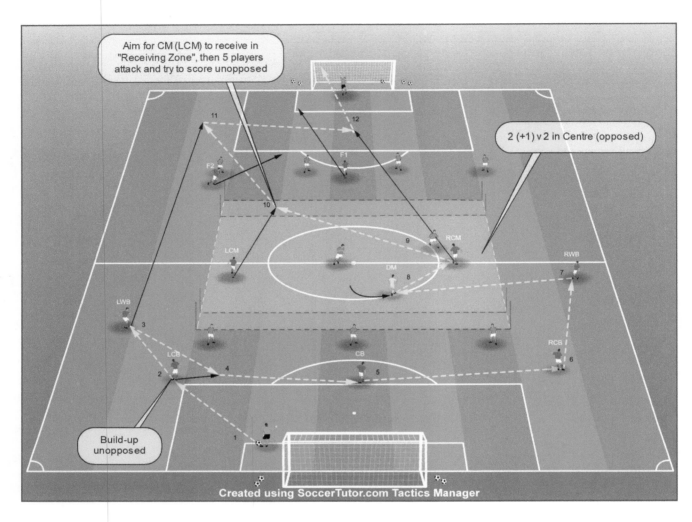

Aim for CM (LCM) to receive in "Receiving Zone", then 5 players attack and try to score unopposed

2 (+1) v 2 in Centre (opposed)

Build-up unopposed

Created using SoccerTutor.com Tactics Manager

Practice Description

- Using a full pitch, mark out a central zone (white highlighted area) + 2 "Receiving Zones" (yellow), as shown.

- The practice starts with the GK playing a short pass.

- The team in possession (blues) build-up play unopposed and then pass to a central midfielder in the white central zone.

- The overall situation is 11 v 3 - only the 2 red central midfielders and GK are active.

- Within the central area, we have a 3 v 2 situation with the yellow joker (**DM**).

- The blues aim is to use the numerical advantage in the central area with help from the defensive midfielder (**DM**) and for a central midfielder (**LCM** or **RCM**) to receive in the "Receiving Zone."

- From there, the central midfielder (**LCM**) tries to play a pass in behind the defensive line and the blues try to score (unopposed) with 4-6 players taking part in the attack.

2 Conditions: Only 2 touches allowed in the "Receiving Zone" (receive and shoot) and the receiver (**LCM**) must arrive there with a forward run/movement and must not already be positioned in there before the pass is played.

5. Build-up Play Through the Lines and Finish in an 11v11 Tactical Game

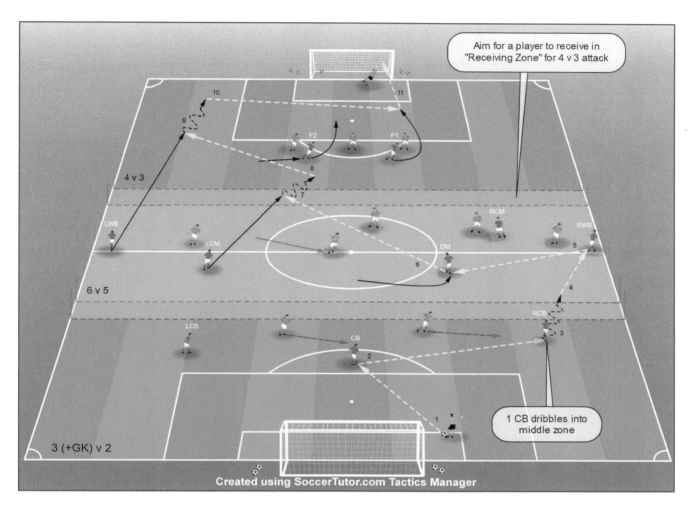

Created using SoccerTutor.com Tactics Manager

Practice Description

- Using a full pitch, mark out a central area (white highlighted area) + 2 "Receiving Zones" (yellow), as shown.

- The practice starts with the GK's short pass to a centre back in the low zone, where the team in possession (blue) use their 4v2 numerical advantage (including GK) to move the ball into the central area.

- The 2 red forwards aim to win the ball and then score within 5 seconds.

- Within the central zone, there is a 6v5 situation, as 1 centre back moves forward (**RCB** dribbles forward in diagram example).

- The aim is to use the numerical advantage in the central zone (6v5) and pass to a player in the yellow "Receiving Zone." The 5 red players aim to win the ball and then score within 8-10 seconds.

- There are only 2 touches allowed in the "Receiving Zone" and the blues have a 4v3 attack (2 players move forward from central zone) in the end zone to try and score.

- The 3 red centre backs try to win the ball and then complete 2 passes between them to score 1 point/goal.

- After each phase, the teams switch roles and the GK of the opposite team restarts.

TRAINING SESSION 3:
SWITCHING PLAY

I. Switching Play in an Unopposed Positional Pattern of Play Warm-up

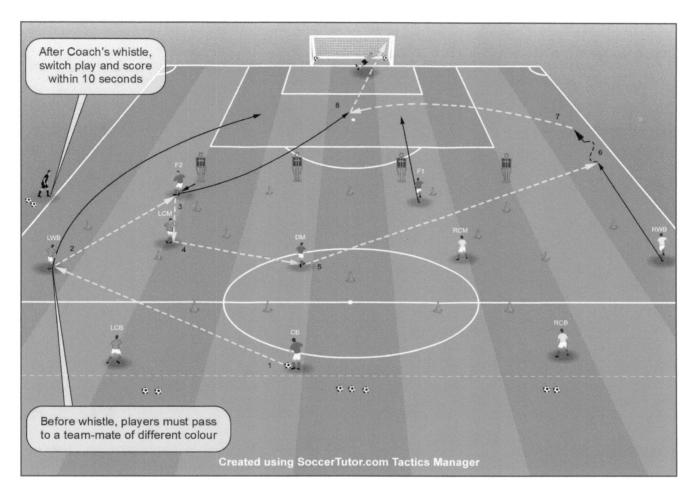

After Coach's whistle, switch play and score within 10 seconds

Before whistle, players must pass to a team-mate of different colour

Created using SoccerTutor.com Tactics Manager

Practice Description

- In the area shown, we have 10 outfield players wearing 3 different colours (red, blue and yellow) and 1 GK.

- Across the pitch there are obstacles (cones) positioned to make every player pass and move within tight spaces.

- The practice starts with one of the 3 deepest players and the ball is circulated with a maximum of 2 touches allowed.

- Initially, the players are only allowed to pass to a player with a different colour shirt.

As soon as the Coach's whistle is blown, which must be when the ball is wide, the players try to score with the following **3 Conditions**:

1. Switch the play to a player on the weak side.

2. If the Coach blows his whistle with a red player in possession, the ball must be switched to a yellow player, and vice versa.

3. Score within 10 seconds of the Coach's whistle.

2. Switching Play in a 3 Zone 8v8 (+2) Possession Game

Practice Description

- In the area shown, we play an 8v8 (+2) possession game, with all players in their specific positions within the 3-5-2 formation.

- Each team has a left centre back (**LCB**), right centre back (**RCB**), left wing back (**LWB**), right wing back (**RWB**), left central midfielder (**LCM**), right central midfielder (**RCM**) and 2 forwards (**F1** and **F2**).

- The yellow jokers play with the team in possession and take up the roles of the middle centre back (**CB**) and the defensive midfielder (**DM**).

- The wing backs are all positioned in the wide zones, with all other players positioned in the central zone - the aim is to switch play from wide zone to the other.

- The wing backs do not contest each other in the wide zones.

Rules

1. Always start from the Coach's pass to the middle centre back (**CB**), which is a yellow joker.

2. The team in possession (blues in diagram) have unlimited touches.

3. A point is scored each time the ball is moved from one side wide to another.

3. Switching Play in a 3 Zone Conditioned Game with 4 Mini Goals

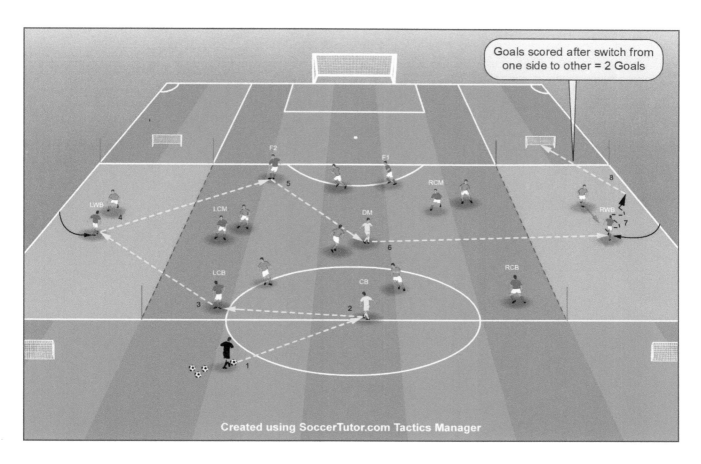

Goals scored after switch from one side to other = 2 Goals

Created using SoccerTutor.com Tactics Manager

Practice Description

- In this progression of the previous practice, we now add 4 mini goals in the positions shown.

- The wing backs are still all positioned in the wide zones and all other players are positioned in the central zone **BUT** now the aim is to switch play from one zone to the other and then score in a mini goal.

- The wing backs are now allowed to contest each other in the wide zones.

Rules

1. Always start from the Coach's pass to the middle centre back (**CB**), which is a yellow joker.

2. **The team in possession** (blues in diagram) have unlimited touches.

3. You can score goals on either side.

4. A goal scored after the ball is moved from one wide zone to the other is worth double (2 Goals).

4. Switching Play in a 3 Zone 11 v 11 Conditioned Game

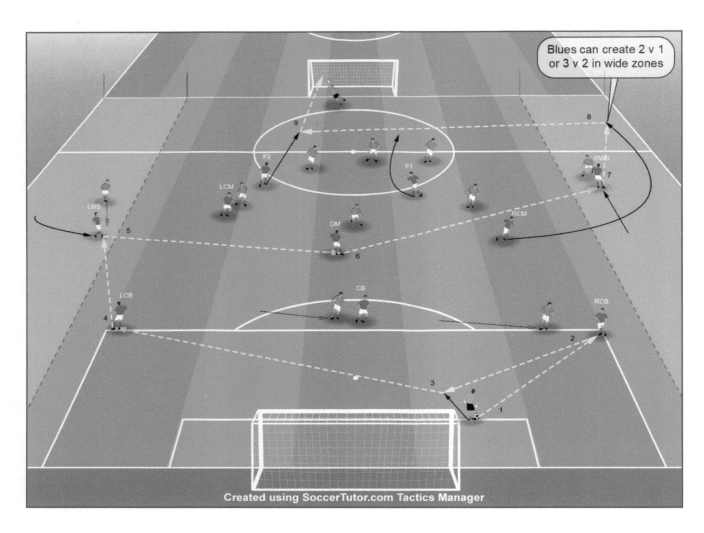

Blues can create 2 v 1 or 3 v 2 in wide zones

Created using SoccerTutor.com Tactics Manager

NOTE: This game is 11 v 11 but you can also play with lower numbers.

Practice Description

In this progression of the previous practice, we now play an 11 v 11 game within a larger area and replace the 4 mini goals with 2 large goals + GKs.

The players play a conditioned game, with an emphasis on switching play.

Rules

1. Always start from the GK.

2. The players have unlimited touches.

3. If 1 blue player enters a wide zone, a 2 v 1 advantage is created and no red players can move in there.

4. If 2 players enter a side zone, 1 red player can enter to create a 3 v 2 situation.

5. A goal scored after the ball is moved from one wide zone to the other is worth double (2 Goals).

Variation - Add a Fast Unopposed Attack

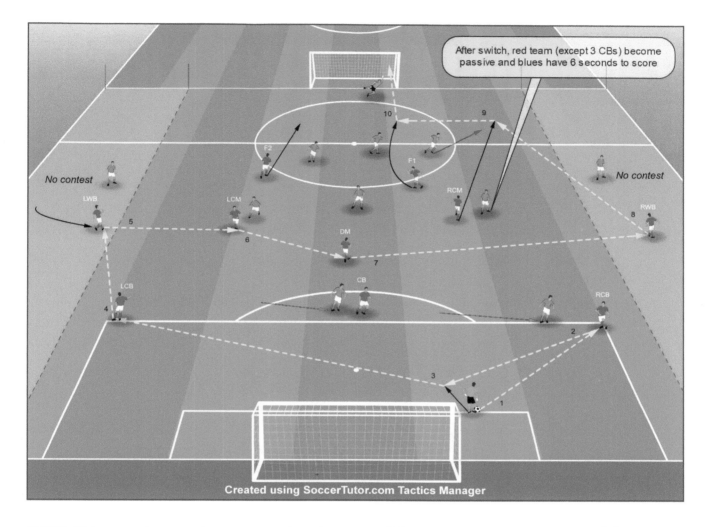

After switch, red team (except 3 CBs) become passive and blues have 6 seconds to score

No contest

No contest

Created using SoccerTutor.com Tactics Manager

NOTE: This game is 11 v 11 but you can also play with lower numbers.

Practice Description

In this variation of the previous practice, the players are still playing a conditioned game, with only the rules changing (see rules below).

Rules

1. Always start from the GK.

2. The players have unlimited touches.

3. If the team in possession successfully move from one wide zone to the other, all of the opposing team's players (except for the 3 centre backs) become passive and are no longer allowed to take part in the game.

4. From the moment the opposing team become passive (reds in diagram), the team in possession (blues) have 6 seconds to try and score. After this 6 seconds, the game starts again from the opposing GK.

TRAINING SESSION 4:
PLAYING IN BEHIND THE DEFENSIVE LINE

1. Attacking Interplay, Playing the Final Pass and Timing Runs in Behind the Defensive Line

Players must pass to a player of different colour

On Coach's whistle, midfielder must play in behind for forward

Created using SoccerTutor.com Tactics Manager

NOTE: This practice has 5 players but you can also use the entire team (see next page).

Practice Description

- Position 4 or 5 mannequins (opposition's defensive line) in the positions shown and many cones, which act as obstacles to force the players to play in tight areas and prevents them from standing still in their positions.

- The practice starts with the Coach's pass to the defensive midfielder (**DM**) and the players circulate the ball. Each pass must be made to a player of a different colour bib e.g. Blue **DM's** pass to the yellow forward (**F1**).

- The blue midfielders pass to either yellow forward (**F1** or **F2**) and they pass the ball back (lay-off) to the blue midfielders.

- On the Coach's whistle, a blue midfielder (**RCM** in diagram) must play a final pass in behind the defensive line.

- Both forwards time their runs in behind, as shown. The one who receives (**F2**) tries to score past the GK.

- The other forward (**F1**) follows up for any potential rebounds.

Progression - Full 10 Outfield Players

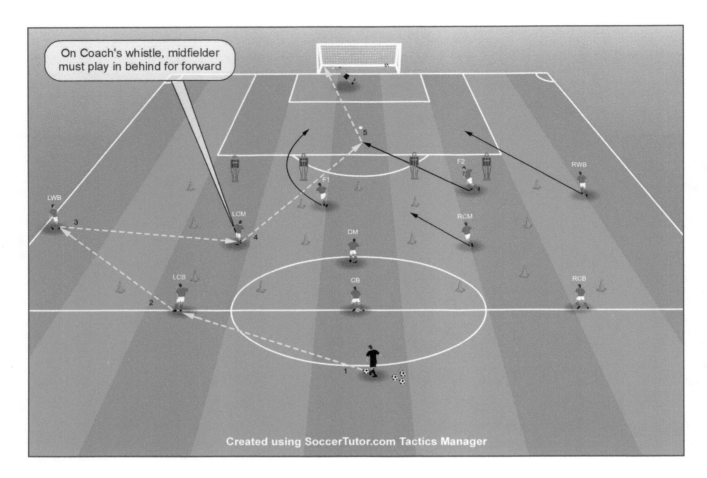

On Coach's whistle, midfielder must play in behind for forward

Created using SoccerTutor.com Tactics Manager

Practice Description

- In this progression of the previous practice, there are now 10 outfield players set out in the 3-5-2 formation wearing the same colour.

- The practice starts with the Coach's pass to a centre back (**LCB** in diagram) and the players circulate the ball.

- On the Coach's whistle, the player in possession (**LCM** in diagram) must play a final pass in behind the defensive line.

- Throughout the practice, the players must take 1 touch and 2 touches alternately e.g. In the diagram, the **LCB** passes with 1 touch, the **LWB** receives and passes to the **LCM** using 2 touches, and the **LCM** uses 1 touch to play a pass in behind the defensive line for the run of the forward (**F2**).

- Both forwards time their runs in behind, as shown. The forward (**F2**) who receives tries to score past the GK.

- The players on the opposite side (**RCM**, **RWB** and **F1**) all make movements to support the attack and are ready for any potential rebounds.

2. Dynamic 7 v 7 (+3) Possession Game + Pass in Behind and Finish

Aim: Complete 6 passes and play final ball

7 (+3) v 7

Created using SoccerTutor.com Tactics Manager

Practice Description

• In the marked out area, there are 2 teams of 7 players + 3 jokers.

• The practice starts with the Coach's pass and the aim is to keep possession.

• The blues must complete 6 passes, then play a pass in behind after a lay-off and score.

Rules

1. The players have unlimited touches.

2. The team must complete 6 passes before playing a final ball (adjust for age/level).

3. Once a team has completed 6 passes, the defending team can only intercept passes and cannot tackle the ball carrier.

4. The defending team players are not allowed to leave the main area to defend.

5. The receiver of the ball can only enter the end zone after the pass is played (offside rule).

6. The receiver must take their first touch in a forward direction, which prevents long passes to a player with his back to goal.

3. Playing in Behind the Defensive Line in a 10 v 10 Game with Receiving End Zones

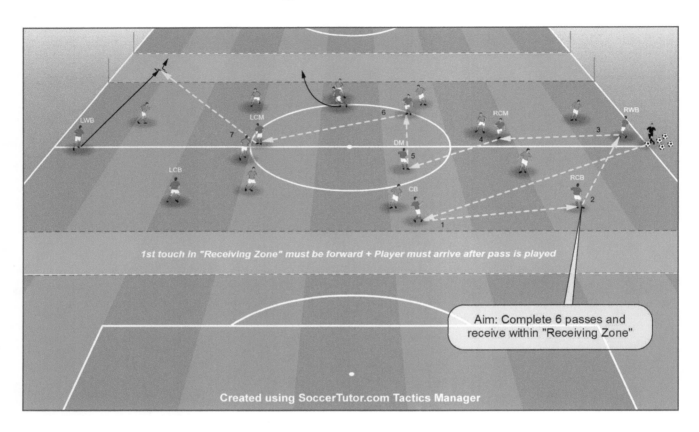

1st touch in "Receiving Zone" must be forward + Player must arrive after pass is played

Aim: Complete 6 passes and receive within "Receiving Zone"

Created using SoccerTutor.com Tactics Manager

Practice Description

- Mark out a main area + 2 "Receiving Zones" (yellow highlighted areas).

- The practice starts with the Coach's pass to a centre back and we play a 10 v 10 game.

- The aim is to build-up, play through pressure and play a final pass for a player to receive in the end "Receiving Zone" (goal).

Rules

1. The players have unlimited touches.

2. The team must complete 6 passes before playing a final pass (adjust for age/level).

3. Once a team has completed 6 passes, the defending team can only intercept passes and cannot tackle the ball carrier.

4. The final pass must be played with 1 touch, but can be along the ground or in the air.

5. Defenders cannot enter the end zones.

6. The receiver can only enter the "Receiving Zone" after the pass is played (offside rule).

7. The receiver must take their first touch in a forward direction, which prevents long passes to a player with his back to goal.

4. Playing in Behind the Defensive Line in an 11 v 11 Conditioned Tactical Game

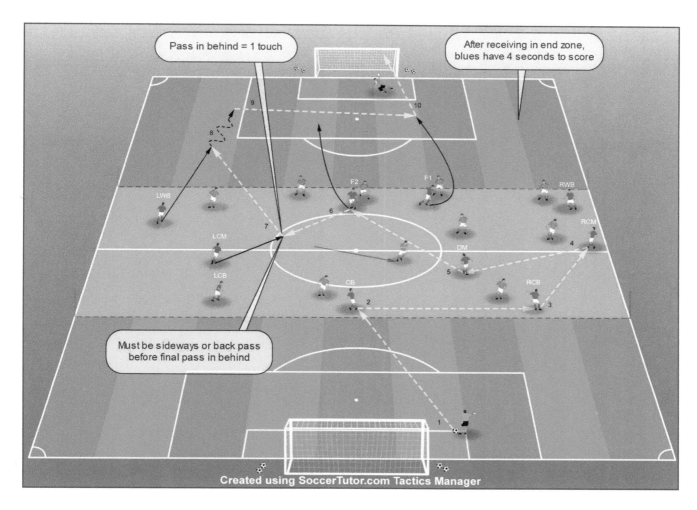

Practice Description

In this final practice of the session, we play an 11v11 game. The outfield players are all positioned within the marked out middle zone, as shown.

The practice starts with a GK's pass to a centre back. The aim is to build-up, play through pressure and play a final pass for a player to receive in behind and score.

To score a goal, the teams have to meet both of these **2 Conditions**:

1. The final pass in behind can only be played immediately after a sideways or back pass.

2. The final pass must be played with 1 touch, but can be along the ground or in the air.

Rules

1. The players have unlimited touches.

2. Defenders cannot enter the end zones.

3. The receiver can only enter the end zone after the pass is played (offside rule).

4. After receiving a pass in the end zone, the attacking team have 4 seconds to score a goal (unopposed).

TRAINING SESSION 5:
COMBINED MOVEMENTS OF THE 2 FORWARDS

I. Combined Movements of the 2 Forwards in a Passing Warm-up

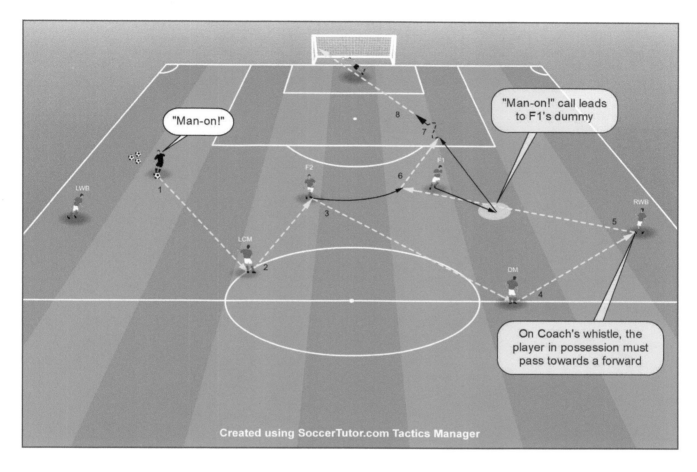

"Man-on!"

"Man-on!" call leads to F1's dummy

On Coach's whistle, the player in possession must pass towards a forward

Created using SoccerTutor.com Tactics Manager

This practice has 6 players but you can also use the entire team of 11 players.

Practice Description

- This is a basic practice to train types of movements necessary for the game development without the presence of opposing players.

- The Coach's pass starts the practice and the players circulate the ball.

- When the Coach blows the whistle, the player in possession must pass to the closest forward (**RWB** towards **F1** in diagram).

- The Coach also calls out "Time" or "Man-on" to determine whether the forward has time to play.

- In this example, the Coach calls out "Man-on" when **RWB** plays his pass, so **F1** knows a defender is close.

- **F1** therefore decides to dummy the pass and let it run to his team-mate (**F2**). **F1** drops back to drag his marker away and then makes a forward run to receive in the space created behind.

NOTE: Please see the analysis on **pages 21 to 28** for different tactical situations and solutions for the "Combined Movements" of the 2 forwards. You can then implement these into the patterns for this unopposed practice.

2. Build-up Play and Combined Movements of the 2 Forwards in a Functional Practice

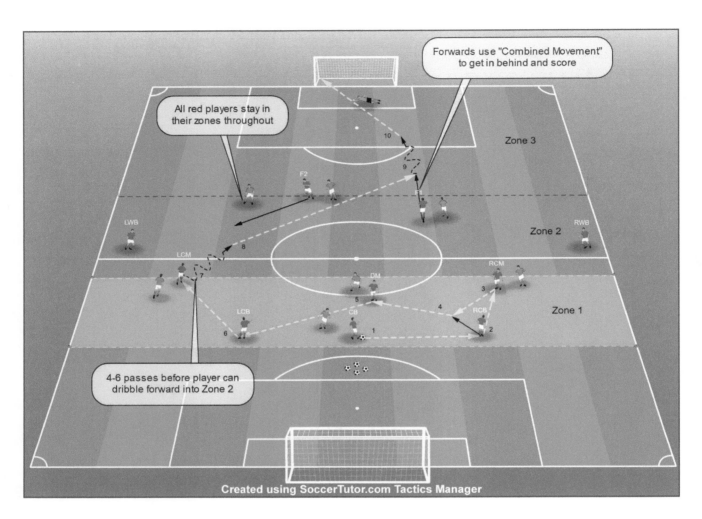

Practice Description

- Using 3/4 of a full pitch, mark out 3 zones as shown. In Zone 1, there is a 6v4 situation, in Zone 2 there is a 4v3 situation and in Zone 3, there is a GK defending the goal.

- The practice starts with the blue team in Zone 1. They must complete 4-6 passes before 1 player (**LCM** in diagram example) is allowed to dribble the ball into Zone 2.

- From there, the blues attack in a 5v3 situation and the 3 red defenders are not allowed to move beyond the Zone 2 line.

- The aim for the blues is to use a "Combined Movement" from the 2 forwards to get in behind and score.

- In this example, the forward closest to the ball (**F2**) makes a movement to drag his marker away from the centre. The left central midfielder (**LCM**) plays a diagonal pass into the space created.

- **F1** receives in behind and tries to score past the GK.

- The practice restarts from Zone 1 with a blue defender.

NOTE: Please see the analysis on **pages 21 to 28** for different tactical situations and solutions for the "Combined Movements" of the 2 forwards. You can then implement these into the patterns for this unopposed practice.

Progression - Defenders Can Defend Deep

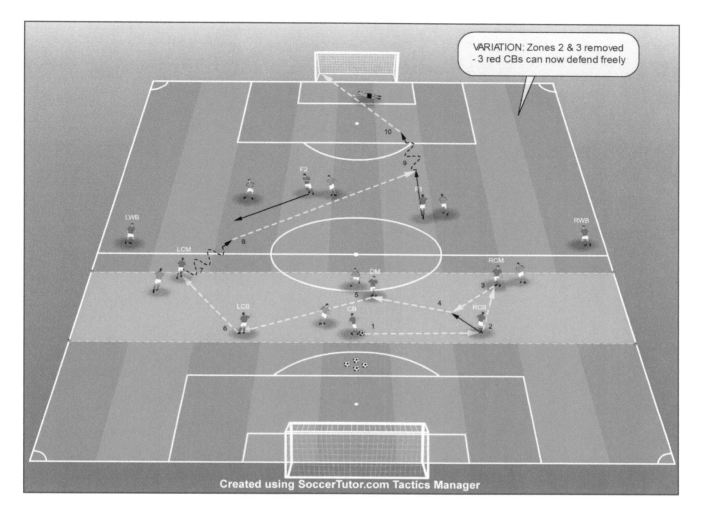

Practice Description

- This is a progression of the previous practice with the only difference being that Zones 2 and 3 are now combined.

- The red defenders are now free to move where they like and defend in deep areas if they want to.

- The aim for the blues is still to use a "Combined Movement" from the 2 forwards to get in behind and score.

- The practice always restarts from Zone 1 with a blue defender.

NOTE: Please see the analysis on **pages 21 to 28** for different tactical situations and solutions for the "Combined Movements" of the 2 forwards. You can then implement these into the patterns for this unopposed practice.

3. Build-up Play and Combined Movements of the 2 Forwards in an 11 v 11 Game with Finishing Zones

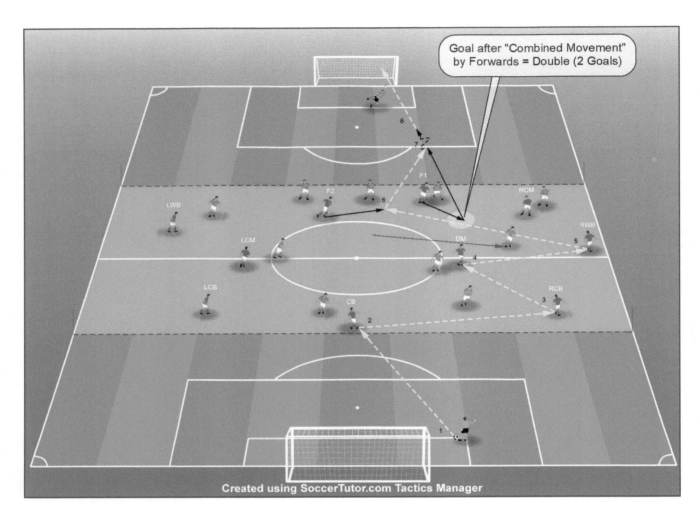

Goal after "Combined Movement" by Forwards = Double (2 Goals)

Created using SoccerTutor.com Tactics Manager

Practice Description

- In this final practice of the session, we play an 11v11 game. The outfield players are all positioned within the marked out middle zone, as shown.

- The practice starts with a GK's pass to a centre back. The aim is to build-up, play through pressure and play a final pass for a player to receive in behind and score.

- Only the player receiving a pass in behind can move outside of the middle zone.

- **KEY POINT:** If a goal is scored by using a "Combined Movement" of the 2 forwards, it is worth double (2 goals).

NOTE: Please see the analysis on **pages 21 to 28** for different tactical situations and solutions for the "Combined Movements" of the 2 forwards. You can then implement these into the patterns for this unopposed practice.

TRAINING SESSION 6: TRANSITION FROM ATTACK TO DEFENCE

KEY POINT

- The transition from attack to defence is not covered in the analysis section of this book, however it is extremely important to practice as an integral part of a team's tactics and performance.

- Therefore, we have provided a training session example for how to train for the transition from attack to defence using the 3-5-2 formation.

I. Possession and Fast Reactions to Losing the Ball in a 7v3 Transition Game with 4 Mini Goals

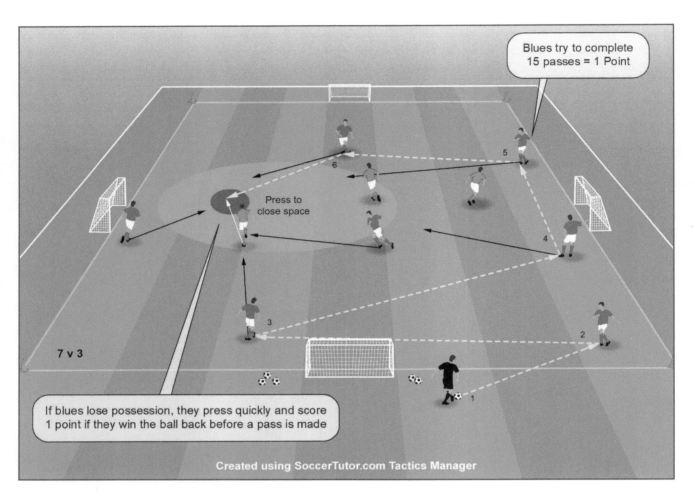

Blues try to complete 15 passes = 1 Point

Press to close space

7 v 3

If blues lose possession, they press quickly and score 1 point if they win the ball back before a pass is made

Created using SoccerTutor.com Tactics Manager

Practice Description

- This is a useful practice to train the immediate reaction to losing the ball. It is not a tactical practice and there is no direction of play - it simply teaches players to immediately press the ball carrier to prevent potential passes and shots, and to win the ball back.

- The size of the area is small (20 x 25 yards) to allow the red players who win the ball to have a mini goal close by which they can score in. This increases the intensity of the blue players' transition from attack to defence.

- The practice starts with the Coach's pass.

- The 7 blue players keep possession of the ball. If they complete 15 passes, they score 1 point.

- When the blues lose the ball, they make a very fast transition from attack to defence and try to win the ball back immediately from the new ball carrier.

- If they win the ball back before the new red ball carrier completes a pass, they score 1 point.

- When the 3 red players win the ball, they score 1 point by completing 4 passes or scoring in any mini goal (after at least 1 pass).

2. Possession and Fast Reactions to Losing the Ball in a 10 v 5 Transition Game with 6 Mini Goals

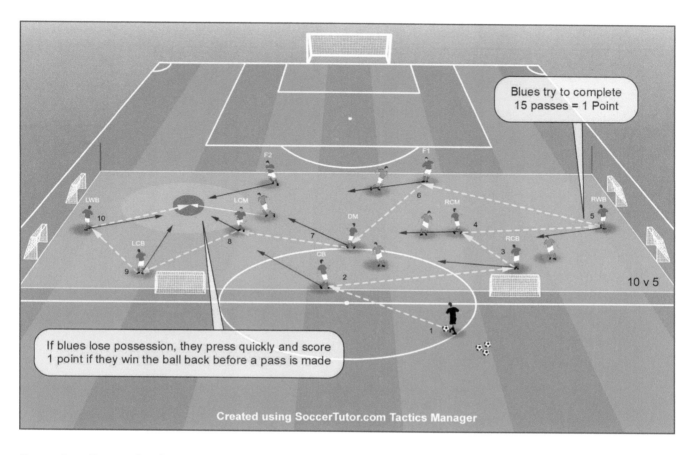

Blues try to complete 15 passes = 1 Point

If blues lose possession, they press quickly and score 1 point if they win the ball back before a pass is made

10 v 5

Created using SoccerTutor.com Tactics Manager

Practice Description

- In this progression of the previous practice, we now add more players and a tactical context to the transition from attack to defence.

- In the area shown, the blue team have 10 players set out in the 3-5-2 formation.

- The 10 blue players keep possession of the ball, with a focus on constant movement to change the angles and provide continuous solutions to the ball carrier.

- If the blues complete 15 passes, they score 1 point.

- When the blues lose the ball, they make a very fast transition from attack to defence and try to win the ball back from the new ball carrier immediately.

- If the blues win the ball back before the new red ball carrier completes a pass, they score 1 point.

- When the 5 red players win the ball, they score 1 point by completing 4 passes or scoring in any mini goal (after at least 1 pass).

3. Fast Transition from Attack to Defence in a Dynamic 10 v 8 (+GK) Game

Practice Description

- Using half a full pitch, the blue team have all 10 outfield players in a 3-5-2 formation.

- The red team have 8 players in a 3-5 formation and a goalkeeper.

- The practice starts with the Coach's pass to a defender and the blues try to build-up play and score a goal past the GK.

- The red team defend their goal and try to win the ball.

- If the reds win the ball, they score 1 point by either dribbling past the halfway line or completing 7 passes.

- When the blues lose the ball, they make a very fast transition from attack to defence and try to win the ball back from the new ball carrier immediately.

- In this more tactical practice, the blue players must also be aware of defensive balance and shape, making sure not to let the red opponents break through them and score any points.

4. Fast Transition from Attack to Defence in a 3 Zone Conditioned Game

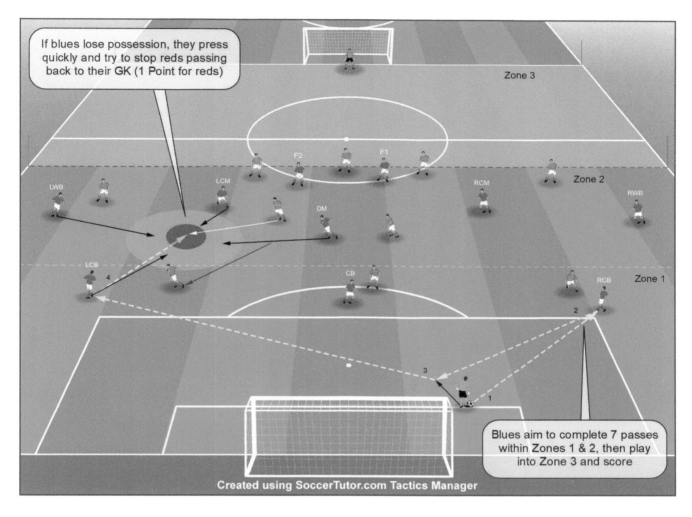

If blues lose possession, they press quickly and try to stop reds passing back to their GK (1 Point for reds)

Blues aim to complete 7 passes within Zones 1 & 2, then play into Zone 3 and score

Created using SoccerTutor.com Tactics Manager

Practice Description

- In 2/3 of a full pitch, mark out 3 zones as shown. Both teams have a full 11 players including GKs in large goals.

- The practice starts with the blue team's GK and the blues play within the first 2 zones.

- The blue team aim to successfully complete 7 passes within Zones 1 and 2, then play into Zone 3 (end zone) and score past the GK.

- The red players can only intercept passes (no tackles) and no red players are allowed to defend in Zone 3.

- If the reds win the ball within Zones 1 and 2, they immediately look for a back pass to their GK (1 point).

- When the blues lose the ball, they make a very fast transition to defence and try to win the ball back from the new red ball carrier immediately and prevent the back pass.

- As long as the reds are unable to pass back to their GK, the blue team actively defend, trying to win the ball back.

- If the blues win the ball back (1 point), restart the game from the blue GK.

5. Fast Transition from Attack to Defence in an 11v11 Conditioned Tactical Game

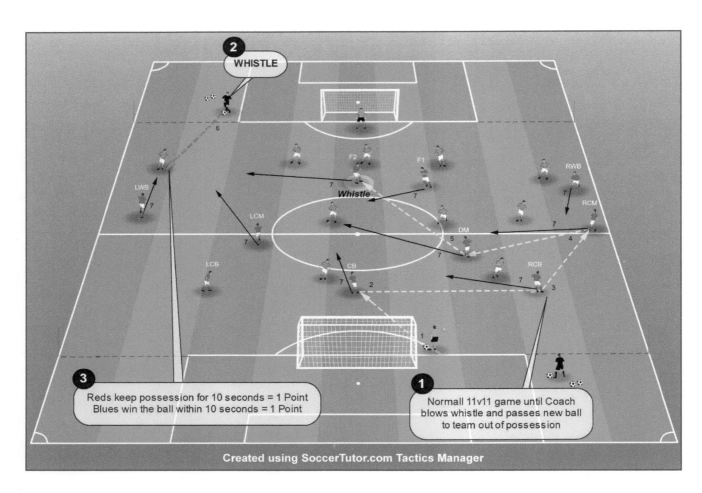

Reds keep possession for 10 seconds = 1 Point
Blues win the ball within 10 seconds = 1 Point

Normall 11v11 game until Coach blows whistle and passes new ball to team out of possession

Created using SoccerTutor.com Tactics Manager

Practice Description

- During the development of a normal 11v11 game, the Coach blows the whistle and plays a new ball to the team out of possession (reds in diagram example).

- The first ball is disregarded and the red team then aim to keep possession of the new ball for 10 seconds to score 1 point.

- The blues make a fast transition from attack to defence.

- If the blues win the ball back within 10 seconds, they score 1 point.

- In addition, after winning the ball back, the reds become passive and the blues try to score a goal (unopposed) for an extra point.

KEY POINTS

- The first 3 practices in this training session are now all inserted into a real tactical context (11v11 game) to recreate various game situations.

- It is extremely important for the transition from attack to defence to be carried out effectively, always maintaining the correct order and distances.

- Whilst the players near the ball area immediately press the new ball carrier and close down and/or block the potential receivers, the other players are compact and recover the correct positions.

TRAINING SESSION 7:
AGGRESSIVE PRESSING

I. Dynamic Transition Game with Goalkeepers in End Zones

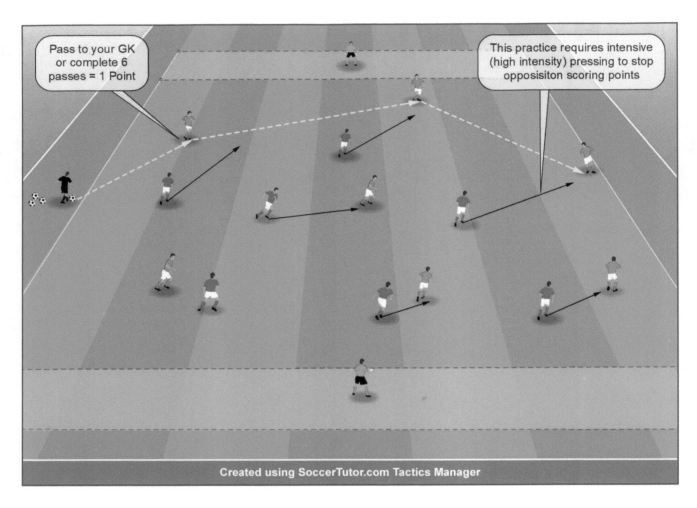

> Pass to your GK
> or complete 6
> passes = 1 Point

> This practice requires intensive
> (high intensity) pressing to stop
> opposisiton scoring points

Created using SoccerTutor.com Tactics Manager

NOTE: To prepare the team to defend using effective aggressive pressing, it is necessary to implement this theme and tactical development into the training sessions and make sure continuous pressing is required.

Practice Description

There are 2 teams of 7 players in the main zone and 1 GK in each end zone - adjust the size of the area to suit the age/level of the players.

The practice starts with the Coach's pass and the team in possession can score points in 2 ways:

1. Pass to your team's GK.

2. Complete 6 consecutive passes.

- Having 2 different ways to score points forces the defending team to constantly press and not simply position themselves to block the path to the GK, for example.

- When a team scores a point, the play restarts with the same team receiving from the opposition's GK.

- In this practice, the defending team is forced to exert continuous pressing on the ball carrier and potential receivers to stop points being scored. Therefore, it is necessary to play in short periods (e.g. 3 minutes), so that the practice is always performed with a high intensity while maintaining the purpose.

2. Aggressive Pressing High Up the Pitch to Stop Build-up in a Dynamic Conditioned Game

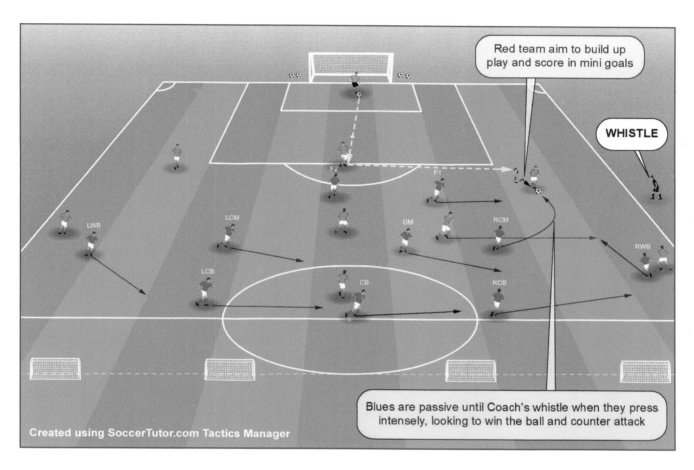

Red team aim to build up play and score in mini goals

WHISTLE

Blues are passive until Coach's whistle when they press intensely, looking to win the ball and counter attack

Created using SoccerTutor.com Tactics Manager

Practice Description

- Both teams are in a 3-5-2 formation, with the reds defending the big goal with a GK and the blues defending 4 mini goals.

- The practice starts with the red team's GK and a short pass to a defender.

- The red team aim to build-up play and score in one of the 4 mini goals positioned 10 yards past the halfway line. They must keep the ball on the ground at all times.

- Initially, the Coach can have the blues press in a "passive way" with the reds using 2 touches. On the Coach's whistle, the practice becomes fully active.

- The blue team aim to win the ball and then launch a quick counter attack.

- **RULES:** The counter attack can be with passive or active opponents. Limit the total number of passes or amount of seconds to score.

KEY POINT

The risk of this practice is that you may teach players to press forward in any situation and not be cautious enough to defend the spaces behind. For this reason, you should alternate this type of practice (mini goals) with practices where the opponents can play long passes in behind.

3. Aggressive Pressing for the Defensive Transition in a Dynamic Conditioned Game

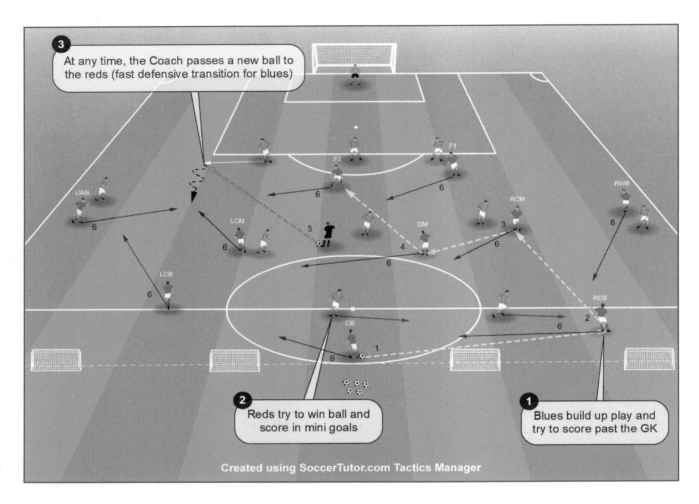

3 At any time, the Coach passes a new ball to the reds (fast defensive transition for blues)

2 Reds try to win ball and score in mini goals

1 Blues build up play and try to score past the GK

Created using SoccerTutor.com Tactics Manager

NOTE: In this practice, the aggressive pressing is applied in the transition from attack to defence. The opposing team (reds) can be in any formation the coach wants e.g. 4-4-2, 4-2-3-1, 3-5-2, 3-4-3.

Practice Description

- This is a variation of the practice on the previous page within the same area.

- This time, the practice starts from the blue middle centre back (**CB**) and the Coach stands in the middle of the pitch.

- The blue team build-up play and try to score in the large goal. The red team try to win the ball and then score in any of the 4 mini goals.

- At the end of a phase of play or at any time, the Coach passes a new ball to the red team and the first ball is disregarded.

- The blue team apply aggressive pressing, trying to win the ball back as soon as possible and stop the red team from scoring in the mini goals.

- The red team must complete 3 passes before they can score.

4. Aggressive Pressing High Up the Pitch in an 11v11 Conditioned Game

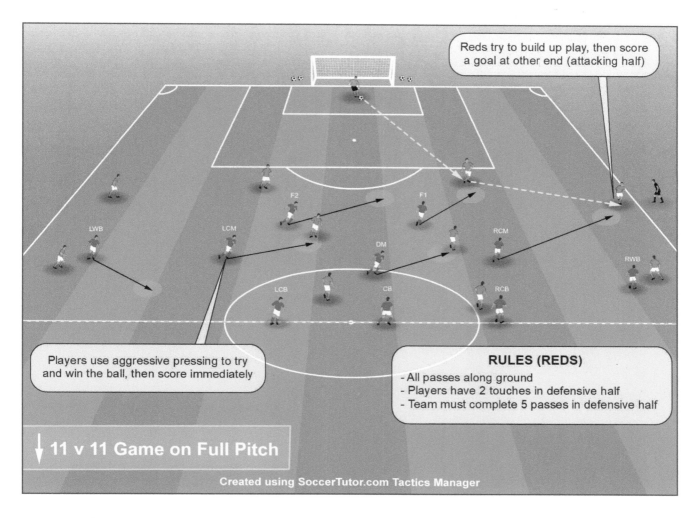

Reds try to build up play, then score a goal at other end (attacking half)

LWB
LCM
F2
F1
DM
RCM
RWB
LCB
CB
RCB

Players use aggressive pressing to try and win the ball, then score immediately

RULES (REDS)
- All passes along ground
- Players have 2 touches in defensive half
- Team must complete 5 passes in defensive half

↓ 11 v 11 Game on Full Pitch

Created using SoccerTutor.com Tactics Manager

NOTE: In this conditioned game, the coach must make sure the players are focussed on the topic of aggressive pressing throughout.

Practice Description

- Using a full pitch, we play an 11v11 conditioned game with the blue team in a 3-5-2 formation and the opposing red team in any formation the Coach wants e.g. 4-4-2, 4-2-3-1, 3-5-2, 3-4-3 etc.

- The practice always starts from the GK and the red team try to build-up play through pressure and score a goal.

- The blue team press high, try to win the ball and then score.

Rules

1. All passes must be along the ground.

2. 2 touches in the defensive half and unlimited touches in the attacking half.

3. Complete 5 passes in the defensive half before moving into attacking half.

4. The pressing team (blues) can score immediately after winning the ball.

5. If a goal is scored or the ball goes out of play, always restart from the GK.

TRAINING SESSION 8:

ORGANISATION OF THE DEFENSIVE LINE

I. Organising the Defensive Line with the Correct Movements and Anticipation (Unopposed)

Variation I - Defend a Forward Ground Pass

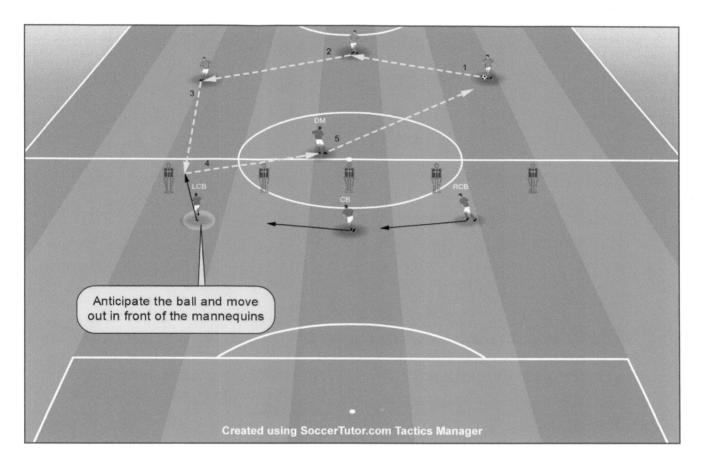

Anticipate the ball and move out in front of the mannequins

Created using SoccerTutor.com Tactics Manager

NOTE: This practice shows just the 3 centre backs with the defensive midfielder, but you can also add the wing backs.

Practice Description (Variation 1)

- The serving players (reds) start the practice by circulating the ball with a maximum of 2 touches.

- The 3 blue centre backs have the 5 red mannequins as a reference, and the focus is on anticipation.

- The focus is on the correct defensive movement and organisation needed depending on the tactical situation.

- The red players use different variations which require different defensive reactions.

- In this first example, the red serving players circulate the ball along the ground until one plays a forward pass in front of the mannequins.

- The closest centre back (left centre back - **LCB** in diagram example) must anticipate the ball and move out in front of the mannequins to receive the pass.

- The **LCB** then passes to the defensive midfielder (**DM**), who passes back to a red serving player. The practice continues.

Variation 2 - Defend an Aerial Pass

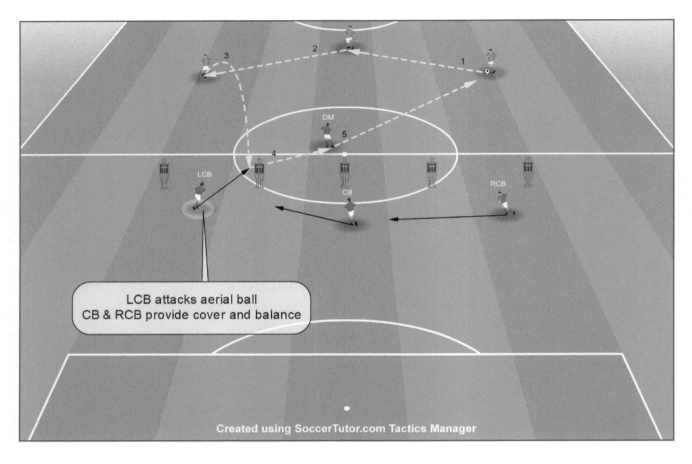

LCB attacks aerial ball
CB & RCB provide cover and balance

Practice Description (Variation 2)

- In this variation, the red serving player now plays an aerial pass.

- The closest centre back (left centre back - **LCB** in diagram example) must anticipate the ball, get to the ball and pass forward to the defensive midfielder (**DM**).

- The other 2 centre backs shift across to provide cover and compactness in the defensive line.

- The defensive midfielder (**DM**) passes back to a red serving player and the practice continues.

Variation 3 - Open Ball Situation

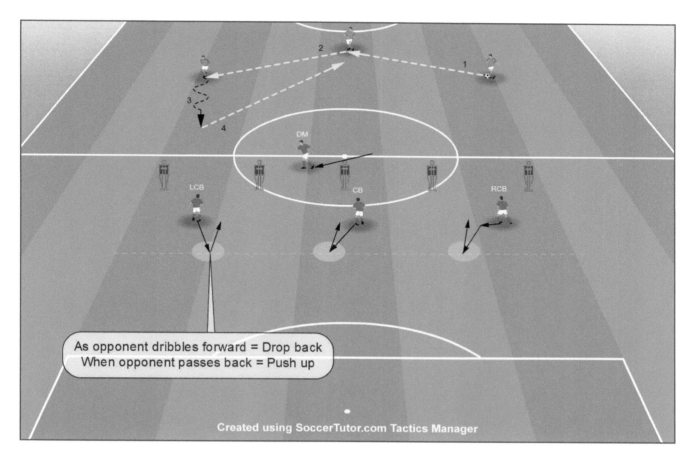

As opponent dribbles forward = Drop back
When opponent passes back = Push up

Created using SoccerTutor.com Tactics Manager

Practice Description (Variation 3)

- In this variation, the blue centre backs practice their collective forward and backward movements to maintain balance in the defensive line, depending on the actions of their opponents.

- After circulating the ball along the ground, one of the red serving players dribbles forward with the ball.

- The **DM** shifts across and all 3 blue centre backs must move back together collectively in a line. This is because the opponent has time on the ball ("Open Ball Situation"), so they must cover the space in behind.

- The red serving player then passes backwards to his team-mate.

- As soon as the ball is played backwards, the 3 blue centre backs quickly push up (move forward collectively) to retain their original defensive line.

- By pushing up, the blue centre backs are able to get closer to their midfield line and enable their team to apply pressure in the attacking half.

Variation 4 - Deep Pass in Behind Defensive Line

CB = Get to aerial ball and pass to DM
LCB and RCB = Cover and balance

Created using SoccerTutor.com Tactics Manager

Practice Description (Variation 4)

- In this variation, the red serving player now plays an aerial pass in behind the defensive line.

- The focus for the 3 blue centre backs is on positioning, quick retreating movements, how to attack the aerial balls and the related balance/cover movements.

- In this example, the middle centre back (**CB**) collects the long aerial pass. He then passes to the defensive midfielder (**DM**).

- The 2 wide centre backs (**LCB** and **RCB**) have also moved back to provide cover and balance to the defensive line.

- The defensive midfielder (**DM**) passes back to a red serving player and the practice continues.

2. Organising the Defensive Line in a Conditioned Small Sided Game

Practice Description

- The blues have 3 centre backs, 2 wing backs, 1 defensive midfielder (+GK) from the 3-5-2. The reds have 4 midfielders and 2 forwards from the 4-4-2, however this can be changed to suit any formation e.g. 4-3-3, 3-4-3 etc.

- The practice starts with the Coach's pass and the red team try to play in behind the blue's defensive line (into the end zone) and score, but they also have specific tactical instructions e.g. Pass wide in 4-2 shape.

- The blue players must make the correct defensive movements depending on the situation - please see the tactical situation variation examples on the next page.

- The blue defenders must adjust their positioning according to the movement of the ball.

- In the diagram example, the blue players practice organising their defensive line when the ball is played out wide against the 4-4-2.

- When the ball is passed wide, the blue wing back on that side (**LWB**) moves to contest the ball. The other blue defenders shift across to provide support/cover, make sure they are compact in the centre and mark the 2 forwards. The wing back on the opposite side (**RWB**) drops back, as shown.

- The practice description continues on the next page...

Practice Description (Continued)

- Whilst making sure the organisation of the defensive line is right and all the correct defensive movements are being made, the blue team try to win the ball.

- In the diagram example, the left centre back (**LCB**) moves forward to intercept a pass. From that point, the blue team have 8 seconds to try and score in either of the 2 mini goals (quick counter attack).

- In the diagram example, the **LCB** passes to the defensive midfielder (**DM**). The **DM** then passes wide for the advanced run of the right wing back (**RWB**), who scores in the mini goal.

- If the reds win the ball back, there is an attempt on goal or the ball goes out of play, always restart the practice with the Coach's pass to the red team.

Tactical Situation Variation Examples

The Coach can give many different instructions to change the tactical situation for the blue defending team. Here are some examples:

1. One of the centre backs moves forward to mark the No.10 against the red's 4-2-3-1, leaving a 2v1 advantage in the centre against the 1 red forward (see page 53).

2. Creating a 3v2 advantage at the back against the red's 3-1-2 from the 4-3-1-2 (see page 85).

3. Defending an "Open Ball Situation" (see page 151).

4. Defending a deep pass in behind the defensive line (see page 152).

NOTE: For more possible examples, please see the analysis section of the book and also add your own tactical situations.

BIBLIOGRAPHY

- C. Albertini, From the concept of play to field exercises. The Barcelona: An example of a systemic approach to training.
Source: www.settoretecnico.figc.it.

- D. Ballardini, The didactics of defence to three, Final thesis of the UEFA Pro course 2000/2001.
Source: www.settoretecnico.figc.it.

- C. Ferrara, The concept of marking in defence to man and zone, Final thesis of UEFA Pro 2007/2008 course.
Source: www.settoretecnico.figc.it.

- M. Giampaolo, The coach's typical week, Final thesis of the UEFA Pro course 2006/2007.
Source: www.settoretecnico.figc.it.

- F. Salsano, The game system of 3-4-1-2, Final Thesis of the UEFA Pro course 2003/2004.
Source: www.settoretecnico.figc.it.

- A. Sottil, The duel. Principles of individual defender tactics, Final thesis of the course UEFA Pro 2012/2013.
Source: www.settoretecnico.figc.it.

- I. Juric, The construction of the game with the form 3-4-3, Final thesis of the UEFA course Pro 2012/2013.
Source: FIGC Technical Sector Library.

- S. Lanna, The phase of not having the form 1-3-5-2, Final thesis of the UEFA course Pro 2013/2014.
Source: FIGC Technical Sector Library.

- E. Capuano, The 3-5-2, Final Thesis of the UEFA Pro 2008/2009 course.
Source: FIGC Technical Sector Library.

- N. Amieiro, Defensa en zona en el futbol, MC Sports, 2007.

- P. Arcuri, We build from below, www.allenatore.net, Lucca 2015.

- T. Athanasios, The trainings of the Barcelona F.C. 160 exercises from 34 tactical situations, Soccer Tutor, 2017.

- A. Bacconi, P. Rossi, La Juve by Antonio Conte. Making the game, Felici, 2012.

- A. Bonatti, The contrasts of 3-5-2. Construction, development and non-construction phases possession to tackle all gaming systems, YouCoach, 2016.

- F. Marziali, V. Mora, Defending on frontal and lateral attacks, Edizioni Nuova Phromos, Città di Castello 2011.

- P. Mendonca, Tac-tac: or futebol de Pep Guardiola periodically, 2015

- M. Silva, O desenvolvimento do jogar, segundo a Periodização Táctica, McSports, 2006.

- Websites consulted:
www.allenatore.net
www.obiettivorganizzazione.it
www.rivistaundici.com
www.settoretecnico.figc.it

Printed in the USA
CPSIA information can be obtained
at www.ICGtesting.com
LVHW062102200224
772322LV00016B/166